FAN IT INTO

Flame

FAN IT INTO *Flame*

FORGED IN FIRE, FUELED BY LOVE

DR. KIMBERLY PAZ-FRAZEE

Take note that the name "satan" and related names are not capitalized. We choose not to acknowledge him, even to the point of violating accepted grammatical rules.

ISBN 13 TP: 978-1-6631-0188-4

FOREWORD

There are stories that inform us, and there are stories that mark us. *Fan It Into Flame* by Kimberly Paz-Frazee is the kind of testimony that leaves a holy imprint on your heart. This book is not simply a memoir—it is a living witness to what happens when a person repeatedly says "yes" to God in the middle of pain, uncertainty, and surrender.

At Warrior Notes School of Ministry, we teach that faith is not proven in comfort but forged in obedience. Kimberly's life reflects this truth with remarkable authenticity. Her journey moves through childhood trauma, addiction, loss, grief, career upheaval, and deep personal refinement, yet at every stage we see the faithful hand of God meeting her. This book reveals that behind spiritual maturity are often unseen years of wrestling, humility, repentance, and perseverance. Kimberly does not hide the hard places—she honors them as the very ground where God's grace took root.

Throughout these chapters, you will encounter a God who speaks—through Scripture, dreams, visions, divine confirmations, and ordinary moments infused with eternal purpose. Kimberly shows us that God is not distant or silent, but deeply personal and intentional. From warnings given before global crisis, to supernatural protection, to quiet lessons learned through family, work, and even caring for birds, her life testifies that nothing surrendered to God is ever wasted. Every chapter reinforces a powerful truth: when faith is mixed with obedience, God releases clarity, healing, and direction.

You will also be encouraged by the way God's work in Kimberly's life overflowed into her family and community. As she learned to listen and obey, God brought healing to relationships, guidance to her household, and hope to children and coworkers through simple acts of love and prayer. This book reminds us that revival does not always look loud, it often looks like faithfulness in everyday assignments.

Fan It Into Flame is ultimately an invitation. It calls you to lay down religious striving, to trust God's voice, and to walk in partnership with the Holy Spirit. It reassures us that transformation is possible, purpose is restored, and eternal impact is released when we agree with God and follow where He leads.

I wholeheartedly recommend this book to anyone who senses that God has been drawing them deeper. May these pages stir what He has already placed within you. *Fan It Into Flame*. Tend it with obedience. And let your life become a testimony of what God can do with a surrendered heart.

Dr. Kevin Zadai
Warrior Notes School of Ministry

CONTENTS

INTRODUCTION

I never set out to write a book.

I set out to survive.

This story isn't about a woman who had all the answers; it's about a woman who cried out in the dark, desperate to find truth, healing, and hope. It's about the God who answered again and again through storms, through dreams, through divine encounters, and through a love I never knew I could receive.

Fan It Into Flame: Forged in Fire, Fueled by Love is the testimony of my life—a life marked by trauma, addiction, healing, and supernatural transformation. This book isn't just for the strong; it's for the broken. It's for the one who wonders if God still speaks… or if He could ever speak to them. He does. And He will.

My prayer is that this story won't just encourage you but will activate something deep inside your spirit. Because what

God has done for me, He wants to do for you. I am nobody special. I am just a woman who said yes. And that yes changed everything.

Chapter 1

A ROUGH ROAD

What did it cost you to get here?

We admire the passion, wisdom, and bold faith of today's spiritual leaders, but how often do we stop to ask what price they paid to arrive at that point in their lives?

Usually, we don't see the lifelong struggle of those who are now serving the Lord with all their hearts, minds, and strength. If you were to poll those people, you would undoubtedly find that most well-known people of faith have had their share of trials and tragedies.

Too often, we see only the polished sermons, confident smiles, and unwavering conviction. What we *don't* see is the pain, struggle, and perseverance behind the scenes. If we looked closer, we'd discover that many of these faithful servants have walked through deep valleys of the shadow of death long before they stood in the spotlight.

Let's reflect on the book of Daniel. Daniel and his three companions were just a small group of boys who were unwilling to compromise their beliefs. They refused to worship any other god but the one true God and were willing to die for what they believed. As the story goes, Yahweh showed up, right on time, in that fiery furnace.

I've been in the fiery furnace—one of my own making. A self-imposed prison. But God was there. He had always been there. My Lord found me in a pit of despair. I had reached a moral and emotional bottom in the summer of 2007 that would require a close encounter of a divine kind to save me.

> *So get yourselves ready, prepare your minds to act, control yourselves, and look forward in hope as you focus on the grace that comes when Jesus the Anointed returns and is completely revealed to you.*
>
> **—1 Peter 1:13 VOICE**

My journey began in 2003 when I walked into a meeting of Alcoholics Anonymous. Having hit my bottom spiritually, mentally, and physically, I was burned out, disgusted, busted, and couldn't be trusted. I didn't even trust myself.

First, let's rewind a bit. In 1972, at age three, my family moved from New Jersey to a small suburban neighborhood on Long Island. It was a tiny, two-story, two-bedroom home. At first, everything was so fresh. I felt excited as we arrived in our U-Haul truck. However, my younger brother was only a few months old or so. And as so often happens to the eldest child, I was no longer the focus of the family. Everyone's attention seemed to be on him; I even noticed a separation between my father and me.

Feeling pushed aside, I spent all my spare time at our neighbors' home. However, what I thought was a haven turned into something I never expected. My parents had become good friends with them and relied on them to babysit me frequently. Unbeknownst to my parents, they begin to abuse me sexually. Both father and son would take advantage of me whenever the opportunity presented itself.

No longer the center of attention at home, I was getting attention at the neighbors' house. Being so young, I could not discern negative from positive attention. No one in my family ever suspected what was really going on with me. My parents had no clue that I was being sexually abused by their best friend.

Two short years later, I started kindergarten and was considered a "more abled learner," as they called it back then. A school counselor picked me out from among my peers and identified me as having an above average IQ. Within a few years, I was in tap, ballet, and Girl Scouts. I even began playing the piano at age nine.

Despite being musical and noticed at school as a stellar student, my neighbors introduced me to alcohol, marijuana, and hallucinogens by the time I was eleven. Even as a preteen, I stayed out all night and ran the streets with neighborhood friends. We would hang out at the local 7-Eleven and smoke marijuana and drink wine coolers. Sometimes there were gatherings in the local parks.

Amid this chaos was church. My mom was a devout Catholic and encouraged my brothers and me to go to church with her every Sunday morning. The church just so happened to be at the end of our street. I never took any of the church activities very seriously, although I did participate in all the rituals and made all the sacraments.

In those days, I knew of a God but didn't know Him personally. I was just performing the motions. My friends and I would go behind the church on weekends and play spin the bottle. Eventually I even stole women's purses during the church services.

The 1970s and early 80s were times of riding bikes and skateboarding. Hip-hop and breakdancing came on the scene. My friends and I were hooked. We would go to nightclubs designed for teens and young adults.

As the years went by, dancing became a priority. My girlfriends and I were in discotheques every single weekend. We would jump on the Long Island Railroad and venture into the Big City to go dancing and see our favorite pop singers perform live.

One weekend we were standing outside Studio 54, all dressed up with fake IDs in hand. My best friend's sister was a bartender there. We would drink all night. Our drive to be in the limelight overshadowed any inherent desire we might have had to do better for ourselves.

While many of my friends were excelling in scholastic endeavors, I was excelling at becoming a neurotic, emotionally insecure degenerate misfit. Sneaking out at night to be with friends became a regular occurrence. This led to many near-death scenarios and scrapes with the law. No matter how hard I tried to be a "good girl," it seemed I was hard-wired for destruction rather than for preservation.

At the age of fourteen, my father noticed the destructive path I was on. He also discovered that one of our neighbors had been exposing himself to me through the window for years. One night I was changing into my nightgown and looked out the window of my bedroom to find him standing out in the backyard and peering in at me. I was petrified.

My dad's reaction to all of this was to move the family further into Long Island to a town called Wantagh. It may have been a small step up the social ladder, but the old neighborhood and all my old friends kept drawing me back. The spirit of rebellion kept me fastened to the old crowd, and I couldn't get loose. Nor did I want to because everyone in the new school treated me like an outcast.

Despite being a party girl, I graduated at the young age of sixteen and left Wantagh High School in 1986. I always endeavored to be an architect, but with such low confidence and zero self-esteem, the best I could get was entrance into a two-year college. At college, I learned I had artistic abilities. I enjoyed the classes, but my interest in boys and in partying would supersede my desire to excel in school. It was nothing short of a miracle that I graduated with my associate's degree in graphic design two years later in May 1988.

Right about this time, my father's employer, Pan American, transferred him to Miami International Airport. We had upgraded neighborhoods. This environment was like nothing I had ever experienced.

I cared more about outward appearances. Diet, exercise, and dating all took priority over school. I was starving myself and taking prescription weight loss drugs along with a host of street drugs. My obsession with losing weight and the pressure to build a sustainable career sent me into a mental breakdown, landing me in the Florida State Hospital by the time I was nineteen.

Any sort of career in graphics or architecture completely evaded me. It took five long months and several prescription drugs before a judge would grant me permission to go home, and that was with strict parental supervision. I lost all hope. My relationship with my father had always been strained. Now he was my guardian, appointed by a judge. Even as a professional pill popper, this was a hard pill to swallow.

My family dynamics drastically changed that year. My youngest brother, Craig, was riding his motorcycle and had stopped at an intersection, waiting for a light to change. A car came barreling down the road from behind and creamed right into him. He broke a leg and an arm, severed a kidney, and had multiple injuries. They admitted him to a pediatric ICU where he would stay well over a month.

During Craig's hospital stay, I watched the nurses closely. What a tremendous impact this experience had on me. My heart bent toward caring for the sick almost immediately. Then, one of the most supernatural things happened. I received a grant from the Florida State Department of Rehabilitation to pay for me to become a licensed vocational nurse. Everything was paid for, right down to my books and uniforms.

Simultaneously, I became pregnant. Being single, I began holding down a job at McDonalds to pay rent.

Only a few months before my graduation, my father announced that he was being transferred to Texas. It had to be Providence that caused my father to be transferred once again. This time it was to San Antonio International Airport.

My daughter, Brooke, was born two weeks before her actual due date, so I had to repeat the entire pediatric rotation to graduate. This meant I would have to leave my newborn baby in the hands of my parents for three long months to finish the entire curriculum. Once I graduated in June 1993, I went directly to San Antonio to join my family and retrieve my daughter.

I lived with my parents for a few months, but after securing a job and an apartment, Brooke and I went off on our own. Being a single parent was challenging, to say the least. I like to tell people that my "picker" was broken. I was always picking the wrong kind of men to date, and it seemed I couldn't not be in a relationship. As it turns out, I was the one who was broken. Really broken. It was only the grace of God that carried me through my twenties and early thirties.

By the time I was thirty-three, I found myself married to an abusive alcoholic. I quickly descended into a pit of despair, and there cocaine became my new best friend. My drinking had progressed to a new and dangerous level. Fortunately for me, hitting rock bottom was the best thing that ever could have happened. While in that pit, face down, with nowhere else to turn and nobody left to confide in, I ultimately reached out my hand to the Lord in desperation.

The cops arrested my husband at the time for physically abusing me. Seeing a marriage counselor was part of his probation in 2003. It astonishes me even today to see how the Lord divinely aligned me to just the right marriage counselor. She directed my husband and I to attend Alcoholics Anonymous (AA). My husband refused to follow this path and eventually abandoned the marriage.

Alternatively, I began attending meetings whenever I could. I tell people I lost a husband, but I gained a higher power. That power was God, hidden in the twelve steps of Alcoholics Anonymous. People who are not familiar with its inner workings often misunderstand the program of AA. I consider myself blessed to have found it along my journey. God undoubtedly set up this situation. "Divine providence," we like to call it. It gave me a way to see and deal with the truth about myself, my circumstances, and the world around me.

> *He drew me up from the pit of destruction, out of the miry bog, and set my feet upon a rock, making my steps secure.*
>
> **—Psalm 40:2 ESV**

Alcoholics Anonymous taught me to seek God in all my affairs and to trust that if my motives were pure, He would answer me. He has done just that! After several years of attending meetings and sponsoring other female addicts, the Lord gave me a desire to seek Him like never before. As AA's "Big Book" says, "We found that God does not make too hard terms with those who seek Him."[1]

By 2011, I had been sober for nine years. I was working as a supervisor at a large research institute and building a new life. Then I met a man who worked there as a paramedic. We started dating, and to my surprise, I soon found out I was pregnant. This came as a shock—not just emotionally, but medically.

Years earlier, my ex-husband and I had tried everything to conceive, including fertility treatments, and were unsuccessful. Now here I was, pregnant again, and unmarried and unsure of the future. Although I was overjoyed, my daughter's father felt overwhelmed. At fifty years old with five children already, he couldn't see himself starting over.

I was heartbroken, but unlike before, I didn't spiral. This time, I had Jesus. I had a new identity. I wasn't the broken girl anymore; I was a woman who could stand firm in her decisions and find grace in her process. I was still attending AA meetings, still working the steps, and now actively seeking spiritual counsel. I learned that healing isn't passive; it requires participation. And I was participating with God every step of the way. It wasn't

1. *Alcoholics Anonymous,* "Big Book," 4th edition (Alcoholic Anonymous World Services, inc., 2001), 46.

easy. There were plenty of emotional ups and downs, especially around my daughter's father. I wanted a family with him.

I had fallen into the trap of being an unwed mother in the past. The enemy thought he had me by repeating the same behavior years later. What he didn't know is that the Lord would come into my life in a mighty way and place my feet on solid ground. Approximately three years after she was born, Kendall's father asked me to marry him.

Then, during a church meeting, someone gave me a prophetic word that pierced my spirit: "The man you want is not the man God has for you. He will never see your way of life." At first, I resisted that truth. But over time, I surrendered. I knew what it felt like to run ahead of God, and I didn't want to repeat that pattern. After many painful years of striving in the wrong direction, I let go.

In 2014, I remember sitting with my AA sponsor at Starbucks. She pulled out her camera and took a picture of me so she could show me what I looked like. She couldn't really explain it, but she said, "You have to believe me when I say you are glowing. You are radiating like the sun."

I didn't think much of it. I was doing my very best to build good character because I had begun dating again. Little did I know, the glow on my face was tied to drawing closer to God. As

I grew more disciplined, His radiance shone through me more clearly.

Granted, I was already in the business of seeking and relying on God, but around this time, I surrendered my will and my life to Jesus at a deeper level. I held nothing back. Having been sober for thirteen years, the Lord placed a desire deep down within my heart to seek Him on an even more intimate level.

Alcoholics Anonymous doesn't corner the market on spirituality, but they sure gave me the start I needed. I had found no group of people who were functioning on that level of transparency anywhere else. In fact, I still haven't. It was like a school for cultivating character. God strategically placed people in my life to guide me onto the path He had already created before I was even conceived. A lifelong pattern of betrayal and disappointments would finally be broken. A supernatural shift occurred in my spirit and in my sphere of influence.

For someone who no longer drank alcohol, it was kind of ironic that I met my second husband in a dance hall. My little brother and I had been celebrating his birthday, and I was only there for that reason. Douglas asked me to dance that evening, and the rest is history. After many years of not committing, I felt that he may be the one. This relationship is what really rocketed me into a higher dimension of existence as I knew it.

By this time in my life, I had made a commitment that everyone who came into my life would be better off for it. I wanted to have the best character I possibly could. After a thorough review of my life, I knew things had to be different going forward and made the decision to not "shack up" with anyone ever again. If Doug was the one, he would honor that decision and respect my choices. Well, the time came, and Doug asked for my hand in marriage. I was a very baby Christian at the time, so I suggested we be engaged for some significant amount of time. Doug and I made the decision to start going to church together, which led to us going for premarital Christian counseling. He immediately put a ring on my finger. Then the challenges really began.

In 2015, I was in a multi-car accident, and I was the target. Two vehicles had hit me from behind during a rainstorm on Halloween. After suffering with horrible pain for two long years, I eventually had surgery on my neck. I didn't know what the outcome would be, and neither did my fiancé. He chose to stick it out with me, and we were married on July 7, 2017.

That number—7/7/17—felt like a divine confirmation. God was doing something new. He was turning ashes into beauty.

Chapter 2

MIRACLES COME FROM PAINFUL PLACES

"Cause of death: chasing a lie sold in a vial of powder."

In March 2018, my brother Christopher died. Heroin didn't just steal his life; it mocked every desperate attempt he made to break free. I watched helplessly, the way someone watches a man drown while holding the very rope that could save him but who is too unsure, too hesitant, to throw it. You see, I had already found my lifeline back in 2003 after surrendering everything to Jesus. I had been practicing the twelve steps of Alcoholics Anonymous for fifteen years.

After losing my brother—my closest friend—grief swallowed me whole. I was drowning in sadness, fear, and despair. But

Heaven was watching. God didn't just see my pain; He moved. He set a chain reaction into motion that shook me awake, jolted my spirit, and ignited something deep inside me that I didn't even know existed.

Can I let you in on a secret? This fire—this awakening—it's just getting started.

When Christopher died, I didn't understand the power I carried. I didn't know that resurrection fire lived inside me. Looking back now, I see things differently. The same power that raised Christ from the dead lives within every believer. It is not a distant hope; it's a living fire placed in us by God. But that fire must be tended, stirred, and kept burning. I know that now, and it's a truth that continues to shape the way I live and the way I love others who are still fighting their own battles.

At the time, we were living in the San Antonio area. We had built a lifetime of memories in that small, suburban San Antonio home. I never imagined leaving; it was all I knew, all I loved. But then my eyes were forced open. The neighborhood around us began to rot; urban decay crept in like a slow, silent disease. The air felt heavier, and the streets were less safe. After our home was broken into for the third time, something in us snapped. We were done. It was time to go.

Because my husband had come from a rural part of Texas, he felt a need to return to that lifestyle. It was a much slower pace than I was used to. Besides feeling out of place, I did not want to leave a home that was already paid for, but my husband discerned this was the right thing to do. We took a leap of faith and began looking for a new home.

After several weeks of searching, our realtor took us to Mico. Doug and I fell head over heels for a one-story, sprawling home nestled into five acres of beautiful trees. It was $100,000 over budget. Not even thinking we could ever afford this property, I received an email from the bank telling me I only had to put 5% down. Then out of nowhere, they increased the loan amount. Soon after, the seller agreed to pay our closing costs.

As these events unfolded, my friends were dumbfounded. They made statements like, "I can't believe that everything is working out in your favor. You must really have done something to please God!" The icing on the cake was when the lawyer I had hired to defend me regarding the car accident phoned me to let me know my insurance company had settled out of court, and he would be mailing me a check for $13,500. It arrived just days before closing and was the exact amount needed.

Against all odds, my husband and I closed on our new home in the Hill Country on March 27, 2018. This was a very big step for me because I would now have to drive an hour to and from work five days a week. I look back on these events now and smile, knowing Jehovah-Jireh was working behind the scenes, and I had no clue.

Our new home was an hour drive from our church in San Antonio, but I had enrolled in Bible college there a year earlier and was determined to complete the course. I committed to driving every Tuesday evening, after work, to class at the church, prior to going home. Those days were very long. I would wake up at 4:30 am to have my quiet time with the Lord. Then came the long drive into San Antonio to arrive at the school by 7:30 am. This discipline took dedication.

It was refreshing to start this Bible class, realizing my pump had been primed for years because of the work I had put into working the AA program. Alcoholics Anonymous is a rigorous journey to mend the broken pieces of your life, with the Holy Spirit as your guide. That was my path to Providence. (Although this way of life suited me, it is not for everyone struggling with addiction.)

Most people have no idea that the twelve-step program is completely taken from the Bible. All twelve steps are based on biblical principles and, when followed correctly, will walk you right into the realm of the Holy Spirit.

Back then I didn't know a simple Bible study would change everything.

What began as a two-year commitment to a local church's Bible study course quickly turned into something much deeper—something life-altering. I was eager for the challenge, ready to dive into Scripture under the guidance of Pastor Matt, who was leading us through the New Testament. Early on, I volunteered to give a three-minute report to the class. It seemed like a small task, plus it came with the bonus of ten extra points on our next test. I had no idea that God had something far greater in store.

While reading through the book of Acts in preparation, I landed on chapter 16—the story of Paul and Silas in prison. I was following along until I reached the moment when the jailer, trembling and desperate, cried out, "What must I do to be saved?" That one question hit me like a flood.

I broke down in tears, unable to hold back the emotion. At that moment, I *was* the jailer. His question was my question. His fear was my fear. I had never before felt such deep conviction. It was the first time I truly placed myself inside the story, identifying with a biblical character not as history, but as personal truth. I was wrecked—and awakened.

That encounter became a turning point in my life. For the first time, I caught a real glimpse of God's mercy and love. It wasn't just theology; it was real, and it was for me. That moment ignited a passion in me to study the lives and hearts of every person in the Bible. What began as an assignment became a lifelong pursuit.

And I haven't stopped since.

Back to that Bible class—the second hour of class was dedicated to the Old Testament. As I dove in, the enemy used every tactic he could to give me more shame, guilt, and remorse about not being able to help my brother. All the blood and goats—there would never be enough livestock available for me to put on the altar. My stress level escalated, intensifying to the point I had incapacitating pains in my head. These headaches began to come more frequently as time went on.

I was focused on the consequences of disobeying a fire and brimstone God. Seeking counsel from my pastors, they really weren't much help. They convinced me that my brother hadn't lived right, and there were consequences to that kind of lifestyle. I was beside myself, thinking we would never be reunited again. I lost a lot of sleep, and the joy had seemed to be sucked right out of me for weeks afterward.

Then God intervened.

I was depressed after losing my brother. I missed his quick-witted humor and his spontaneity. He was always up for a movie or dinner out. Therefore, I poured myself into my program. That was what I had been taught to do. Fellowship and more fellowship would cure my blues. Well, it just so happened that the neighborhood where my husband and I had just bought our new home had an AA meeting only a few miles away. It was my habit to attend twice a week. This one particular evening, I met a man there who shared he too had a brother who died from an overdose. Feeling like I had finally met someone who knew what I was going through, we exchanged phone numbers.

I should have known better.

At first, it seemed so harmless. We began talking on the phone all the time. He would quote Scripture, and I always felt better after speaking to him. But I was seeking solace from another man. He came to church with my husband, me, and our children. We even considered renting our trailer to him to generate extra income. This was the enemy's last-ditch effort to get me off my path.

This man and I formed unhealthy soul ties as we developed feelings for each other. It never progressed to anything physically; however, I'm sure the enemy thought this was his ace in the hole.

I had overcome everything else—drugs, alcohol, food addiction—only to find out there was something called Love Addicts. I had explained this situation to another friend from AA (an ex-priest, I might add), and he suggested that I attend a meeting of Love Addicts Anonymous. What in God's green earth? I was really taken back at that suggestion. Yet, something inside of me felt it was the right thing to do.

Mind you, I was still attending church and going to Bible college. It just goes to show that you can be doing everything right on the outside and still be very misdirected on the inside. We always think we are further along on our spiritual journey than we really are. This is our ego's attempt to rebuild itself. I decided to attend a meeting that very same week.

That first meeting was an eye-opener. These people were speaking my language. In my heart, I did not want to destroy my marriage. I really had to search myself to find out what deep-seated roots I had and then pull them out, from root to branch. This required the help of someone who had been through it, and I needed God.

The program promises that you will be amazed before you are halfway through. Let me testify to what God did for me. I had been working diligently on an inventory that my sponsor gave me. I did a lot of writing. I committed to writing thirty minutes every night. I had to get down to causes and conditions. This was where the rubber met the road. Once I had everything laid out on paper, I began sharing these intimate details with my sponsor. Getting honest with God and another person has always been the key for me to freedom.

One of the first principles I had placed on my inventory that I found questionable was, “wives, submit to your own husbands” (Eph. 5:22). That really bothered me. I had been independent for so long that the thought of submitting to anyone brought about feelings of dependence and weakness.

One night, I dreamed of a large golden hand with its first finger pointing outward, encased in a clear box, like a museum exhibit. A few weeks later, I saw the same image on Facebook, posted by one of my daughter’s friends. I called her, and she told me it was from a statue in Bryant Station, Houston. Its inscription read “Gen. 3:16.” That verse, “I will greatly multiply your sorrow… your desire shall be for your husband, and he shall rule over you,” struck me deeply. It felt like God was speaking directly to me, just as He had to Eve.

That moment marked a profound awakening in me, instilling the fear of the Lord and changing me forever. It was a loving, yet powerful correction. Little did I know the Lord was revealing Himself to me through revelation. That was the catalyst that drew me into covenant with Him. From then on, my steps were easier. Behind the scenes, my husband sought counsel from church elders, whose prayers I believe played a role in my transformation. I can't take credit for the change; it was God, stepping in when I was sinking.

It took years to rebuild trust with my husband, but I'm grateful he never gave up on me. God never gives up on us. Now, I run to Him for guidance every morning. I know that on my own I am nothing—a truth that is now engraved on my heart. Choosing to follow God's ways rather than my carnal ways marked a huge turning point, not only in my marriage, but also in my relationship with the Father. Once He saw my true commitment to Him and my family, He began opening doors and releasing blessings I had no idea were in store for us.

Once I allowed my husband to be the spiritual leader in our family, all sorts of signs, wonders, and miracles began happening for us as well as for the people God was strategically aligning us with. The sacredness of our relationship began to bloom. What once seemed like a thorny patch grew and transformed into firm bedrock, almost overnight.

One treasured moment I look back on is when I had fallen and bent my finger and could no longer wear my wedding ring. I was driving to church one day, and I looked down at my finger. It had become very important to me to wear my ring because that was a symbol of my eternal covenant with God and my husband. I said to myself, "I can't wear my ring anymore because of the fall."

A very small voice in my spirit said, "The fall is what separated Me from My bride too." It was a gentle reminder of how the Lord wants us to return to our first love. This was another one of those "ah ha" moments when I heard the Spirit speaking to me loud and clear.

Our home was becoming a safe haven, a shelter from the storms of life. Together, we were stewarding something beautiful.

In April 2018, a severe thunderstorm awakened me. The wind had blown over a lantern outside, shattering its glass. The clock read 2:00 am. I got up to use the bathroom and felt the entire house shaking on its foundation. I quickly ran and jumped back into bed, falling back asleep.

A bit later, a tremendous turbulent wind in my bedroom woke me up. I gazed at the clock to see it was now 3:00 am. I noticed my husband was sleeping, and his back was turned to me. The wind picked up so strongly that all the papers and folders on our desk were blowing all around the room. I felt the wind blowing on my face so powerfully that it was causing my skin to ripple in waves.

I had no time to think, but I could sense we were not alone. I looked up toward the ceiling, only to realize it was gone. I was staring out at the universe, stars and all. I then noticed five large pink orbs that were floating off to the right, way up high in the night sky. They seemed to be luminescent yet transparent at the same time. Whether I was in the body or out of the body, I do not know. I sat up in my bed, and as I did, I tried looking to my left. A blinding white light, like the brightness of a blinding sun, was there. As hard as I tried, my head would not allow me to look directly at it.

The wind was still so forceful. All I could muster up was, "Chris, is that you?" I can laugh now because it seems so ridiculous for me to have said that. It felt as if a heavy weighted blanket gently pressed me back into my bed, leaving me unable to move or even shift. I melted into the mattress as if I were hot wax, drifting quickly into a deep sleep.

I woke up the next morning very bewildered. None of the papers were on the floor. My husband didn't recall a thing. I took notice that my headaches had subsided. That day we were having two men from our church over to paint the interior of our home. In casual conversation, I told them what had occurred the night before. I will never forget one man's response. As he stood on a tall ladder painting, he looked down at me and stated, "You are going to do mighty works for the Lord!"

I held that visitation close to my heart and only shared it with my husband until now. I had no paradigm for what had occurred. That was the last time I ever felt the pain of those severe headaches. They have not returned, and I believe they never will.

As the summer of 2020 ended, I was returning to my role as a school nurse, a position I'd held for eight years. Over the years, I'd made many friends at the school. One day, a dear friend of mine, Stephanie, walked into the clinic. She asked if I had ever seen the show "It's Supernatural" and shared a bit about it and its host, Sid Roth. Boy, was I hooked. I began watching the show every chance I had. Little did I know, God was preparing me for what was to come. These people Sid Roth interviewed were fascinating. God certainly had been visiting many of his guests. It just so happened that I stumbled onto an episode in which Jesse Duplantis was telling his testimony about the time God visited him in his bedroom. I believe I had to hear this story to realize what had happened to me that windy night in April.

So now, God has really got my attention. I had already been seeking Him regularly, telling Him all my plans and dreams. Do you know what happens when we plan? God laughs! I'm sure of it.

> *"For I know the plans I have for you," declares the Lord, "plans to prosper you and not to harm you, plans to give you hope and a future."*
>
> **—Jeremiah 29:11 NIV**

Chapter 3

GIVEN A NEW LENS

Plunging headfirst into the unknown, I devoured every broadcast on the supernatural I could find. I consumed pages of Scripture as if they held the secrets of the universe. At first, it was something I did so I could pass those hour-long exams. Deep down, I knew it was something bigger. God was revealing the path, showing me the things I was meant to step into. And yet, I craved more. There was a hunger inside me, a burning conviction that there was something more waiting to be discovered.

That same year, a friend whom I had met at church invited me to Dallas, Texas, for a Christ for the Nations conference. I was skeptical at first. I didn't know her very well. However, the title of the conference resonated with me: "The Voice of Healing."

I had said a small prayer before dinner one night while sitting alone in a Luby's diner. "Lord, please show me if You would like me to go to this conference." As I glanced down, a large rainbow came across my table. This was no ordinary rainbow, though. The colors were so intense, like nothing I had ever seen. I knew in my spirit this was a confirmation from God that I should go to the conference. I called my friend, Carol, and I said, "Let's do it!"

We had a great time. We met some great people whom I still stay in touch with. During the first session, the speaker, Todd White, described a detailed vision of a car accident. He even got down to the color of both cars involved. This blew my mind. He was sharing a word of knowledge about the car accident I had been in a few months earlier. He declared healing, and I received it. Back then, I had no idea what a word of knowledge was. Was I about to find out!

The next speaker, Nathan Morris, was walking down the aisle and touched my forehead as he was passing by. I flew back into my seat violently. Expecting pain, I got up and felt fine. I had no earthly idea what this evangelist had transferred to me that afternoon.

On the last day of the conference, a woman asked if she could touch my head. I said, "Sure." When she put her hand above my head, a lightning bolt went through my skull and ran all the way down to the tips of my toes. This jolt sent me flying five feet up off the ground. The girl I had been holding hands with flew about fifteen feet across the stage and was laid out for the next two hours. I didn't know at the time what had occurred. I had no way of processing any of this. All I remembered was that the atmosphere was so thick and felt so holy. How was it that I was able to see the electricity fill the room? It was definitely a sign that made me wonder. Thank God for that woman's obedience!

> *He covers his hands with the lightning and commands it to strike the mark.*
>
> **—Job 36:32 ESV**

A bit later, the same girl said to me, "God says you are pretty. He loves your smile. You are very wise." Although shocked at her comments, I went on worshiping and dancing in the crowd like everyone else. I didn't realize it then, but something had been deposited in me that weekend. Looking back now, I believe it was the fire of God. I know now that I was marked for intercession.

My husband arrived that Saturday afternoon so we could drive directly to Rowlett, a small suburb of Dallas. My aunt was having a party where we would see relatives we hadn't seen in many years. We had a great time, visiting and sharing stories with each other. I took a few pictures of my closest cousins. My husband and I drove home to Mico that evening.

Still being so excited about what had occurred at the conference, I had a dream that night of being shown a high-rise apartment. As I went on the tour, I noticed the realtor had long flowing brown hair. He was dark-skinned. He handed me an open-faced sandwich. I looked down and noticed there was a large red slice of tomato on the top. The man then looked at me and said, "Wait," then he poured a large packet of tiny white seeds onto the tomato. I immediately gobbled it up.

I had no hesitation at all. That was not just any man; that was Jesus. This was the first of many dreams I would have in the coming months. I had to write them all down so I could remember them. I began keeping a dream journal by my bed. I would always pray for God to reveal their meanings. I began researching corresponding Scriptures. Watching John Paul Jackson's "Dreams & Mysteries" show became my favorite pastime.

The parable of the sower is what came to mind for this dream. Jesus poured His seeds into my hands, and I ate them. Jesus was a seed. He was telling me to eat of Him. My soil had been well prepared to receive Him. He was pouring Himself out in abundance. What I came to realize was that He had planted a garden deep within my heart.

Now, I must be completely transparent here. I had no idea what was happening. It would take months and even years for me to accurately discern what I was seeing. Even today, mysteries continue to unfold even further. One of my favorite sayings is "Wise men still seek Him." The more I read the Word of God, the more I perceive and believe.

The next night, I had another dream. I was walking down a beautiful tree-lined street, with cars parked along both sides. What caught my attention were three bright red racing stripes running up and down the street. As I looked closer, I heard a voice repeat, "By My stripes you were healed!" three times, each time with more power.

On the third night after the conference, I dreamed again. I entered a church through a side door, and I was wearing a long white robe speckled with gold. As I stepped inside, something like thick honey—or maybe a golden rope—poured over my head and down my neck. The substance had such a powerful effect, I began to shake violently, as if it was propelling me through the crowd. I instinctively began laying hands on people, eager to spread this energy. As I moved through the congregation, I noticed a toddler dressed entirely in blue to my right and a priest in front of me. Feeling an urgency, I picked up the child and rushed out of the church. Stepping into the street, I was amazed to see fruits of every kind falling from the sky, filling the street as rushing river rapids flowed over and around them. I couldn't contain my excitement as I gathered up all the fruit I could hold. For a moment, I wondered what I could do with it all, before deciding to place it in a basket and offer it back to the Lord. Then the dream ended.

I had no earthly idea what these three dreams meant at the time. Revelation is when the Spirit of God and the Word of God come together. It's like two worlds collide. Even now, I still receive more revelation about them. God is incredible that way. There are so many layers of revelation to be understood about any given subject because everything is from Him and for Him. The little boy in the dream represented the ministry I had birthed that was still young and had to grow. That which God had birthed through me was still in its young stage. I had to take hold of it and run with it. The little boy wore blue, a color symbolizing revelation and communion with God. Since then, the spirit of revelation has been unfolding like never before. The fact that I had to pick up the toddler and run out of the church, away from the priest, indicated to me that I would have to break out of the four walls of the church and leave my old religious beliefs behind.

The next day was Monday, so I headed off to work as usual. When I walked into the building, I began seeing boxes of various fruits piled up to the ceiling. As I turned the corner to enter the clinic, I could see boxes lined all the way down the hall. I walked down to the opposite end of the hallway and turned the corner, and still there were more boxes of fruit piled there. It turned out there was a food drive being conducted that day at school. I just looked in awe and thought *Wow, what a coincidence.* Well, that was no coincidence. That was God-ordained.

The very next day while attending Bible college class, my pastor, who usually taught the Old Testament, stepped forward with a serious expression, and while staring straight at me said, "I don't know why, but the Spirit is prompting me to share this: 'You did not choose Me, but I chose you and appointed you to go and bear lasting fruit, so that whatever you ask in My name, the Father will give you. This is My command: Love each other.' John 15:16."

I almost fell out of my chair! Did the Lord just give me a Scripture? Was He letting me know that the dream was specifically from Him? I had no idea that the God of the universe even knew who I was. I was so shocked by this, I started thinking, praying, and seeking Him like never before. The hope and inspiration I felt would propel me into another realm of existence I have now come to know as fire—and not just fire, but holy fire.

Until now, I had been talking to God, learning about God. But this time, He became personal. The Creator of the universe was giving me personal messages. No one can dispute that. I saw what I saw, and I heard what I heard. This let me know immediately that I was on His radar. This meant I would really have to fetch myself up sharply. Something happens to your moral compass when you know God has His eye on you. Being prone to exaggerating, I suddenly would have to keep every detail to its truest form, no longer at liberty to bend the truth. I felt compelled to become as honest and transparent as I possibly could, with His help, of course.

> *The Spirit of the Lord will come powerfully upon you, and you will prophesy with them; and you will be changed into a different person.*
>
> **—1 Samuel 10:6 NIV**

Later that week, I was looking through my camera at the photos I had taken at my aunt's party. I noticed that the images of a few of my relatives were distorted. One half of their body was big, and the other was normal. Two women had their heads caved in. The Lord told me that they were double-minded and spiritually sick. Ironically, it wasn't long after that, they would all stop communicating with me.

This is where I began experiencing the "suddenlies" of God. That very same week, I woke up hearing, in an audible voice, "God heals fibromyalgia!" It was a loud voice that thundered through my belly. Shaking in my bed, I turned to my husband and told him what had happened. He reminded me that his best friend's wife was suffering with this condition. Having worked for a rheumatologist in the past, I had always chalked up this medical diagnosis as "incurable." Chronic pain and fatigue characterize fibromyalgia, yet there is not one diagnostic test to prove its existence. Somehow or another, it has been linked to physical and emotional trauma. Isn't that like the devil!

The very next week at Bible college class, my girlfriend told me she was suffering and in a lot of pain. I asked her why, and she told me she had been diagnosed with fibromyalgia years earlier. Wow! Was this the person God had in mind? Having just returned from the healing conference, I felt angry because she was so kind and didn't deserve that diagnosis. How dare that devil hurt my friend! I felt so empowered at that very moment. I asked her if she wanted to be healed. She said yes! We walked out into the parking lot. She had parked her van right in front and asked me if it would be okay if we got into her van, so I agreed.

She settled into the driver's seat and turned to face me. I was in the passenger seat, locking eyes with her. Without hesitation, I said, "Spirit of infirmity, I command you to leave now in the name of Jesus." As I spoke, a thick, dark mist rose from her chest and dissipated into the air.

"Did you see that?" she asked. I nodded, confirming what we both had witnessed. Then, without missing a beat, we walked back into the chapel classroom, as if nothing had happened, and resumed our Bible study. *Whoa! Is this really happening?* I thought to myself.

Having witnessed it plenty of times that weekend in Dallas, I believed if I said those words, God would come through. I began looking for opportunities to use my newfound gift on anyone who would allow me to. Being a school nurse gave me one opportunity after another to practice. Never in my wildest imagination would I have believed that God was building a healing ministry within me and through me. Somewhere along the line, the whisper of my unspoken "yes" had been captured by the very heart of the Father.

The next week, as I was driving up to the school where I worked, I heard a song on the radio called "Way Maker."[2] I really liked it and began singing it at the top of my lungs as I was walking into the building. I had never heard this song before that morning. When I got to the clinic, the social worker followed right in after me. I had just turned on my computer as I did every morning. She stooped down and found Sinach singing "Way Maker" on YouTube. I asked if she had heard me singing the song moments earlier. She said no but invited me to a concert

2. Sinach, songwriter and artist, "Way Maker," 2015.

at a local church after work where Sinach would be performing. I couldn't believe it.

Coincidence? I think not. Only "God incidents" in my life. I know I was meant to be there. As the singer performed, I could feel the weight of the lyrics penetrating my soul and spirit. At that very moment, I realized that music directed to the Father was a very powerful battle strategy—a strategy I would come to use very often in the months and years that followed.

Chapter 4

A DIVINE ALIGNMENT

Did you know that we sleep for one third of our lives? And one third of the Bible is devoted to dreams.

In June 2019, I was sitting on my sofa, when I felt a wind come through and blow by me ever so lightly. I looked up and saw what appeared to be a long file cabinet fly open like an accordion. Twenty or so long-forgotten dreams started to pop up, as if my mind had filed them away in its recesses. I knew exactly what they were when I saw them. This vision sparked more curiosity and fire in me than before.

Later that same day, I got into the car to go pick up my daughter from a friend's house and was rear-ended by a young girl who wasn't paying attention. The impact was huge, and what it did to my lower back was even worse than what I dealt with from the first wreck I had in 2015. What seemed like really bad luck turned out to be another attempt by the enemy to ruin my physical health and steal my destiny. But it was too late. The unquenchable fire of God had already begun burning deep within me. A freight train couldn't have stopped me from my holy pursuit. I learned to tolerate the pain and believed God is still the God who heals today.

Shortly after the conference in Dallas, I was watching Sid Roth's show one morning, and he introduced Dr. Kevin Zadai. Dr. Kevin had died for about forty-five minutes during a routine dental procedure and was talking to the audience about his experience. I will never forget the black vest he wore as the Lord explained how the words that had been spoken over him had created a false identity. What a powerful segment it was. I remember going to an AA meeting and sharing it with the group. He had to die so God could show him a higher perspective. How blessed we all felt to be given that higher perspective without having to die physically. Though, we did all have to die to ourselves. That is kingdom principle number one—and easier said than done!

A few weeks after attending the conference in Dallas, I fell asleep on my couch and had a dream. In it, I was riding through the sky in a red convertible Volkswagen Beetle, inside a huge coliseum. As I looked down into the audience, Popeye the Sailor Man jumped up, but I noticed that his head was ten times bigger than his body. He pointed at me and shouted, "The spirit of poverty is leaving now!" Then I saw a man walking down a grassy trail. He came upon what appeared to be a garage door, except it was glass. He opened it up and invited me into the space. Then I woke up.

I looked over at the television, seeing a man walking down a grassy trail and opening up a glass door entrance. It was Dr. Kevin Zadai standing in front of his studio in Destrehan, Louisiana. This dream sparked my curiosity.

The following Sunday at church, I prayed for one of the associate pastors. I looked down and saw he was wearing a pair of socks with Popeye on them. The only conclusion I could come up with is that Popeye is married to Olive Oyl. Oil ("oyl") is a common theme in the Bible. I kept an open mind because I know the Lord will always bring everything into focus for me if I remain open-minded and willing. After doing some research on the Volkswagen Beetle, I read that this model had a new navigation system. God was navigating, but would I follow?

That same week, I dreamed of being seen by an optometrist. My vision had been clouded at first. Whoever was conducting the visit adjusted the lenses of both sides so that I could see clearly. Then the two sides converged in the center and my sight was crystal clear. Clarity, insight, and fresh vision were being imparted to me. Not long after this dream, the Lord revealed to me how, for years, foods and medications were designed to cloud our pineal gland. I believe He supernaturally decalcified my vision in this encounter. It was no shock to me when Dr. Kevin Zadai titled a new study guide *Spiritual Discernment: It's Time for an Eye Exam* (2022). I had received mine, just in time.

Later that week, I was soaking in a hot bath, letting the heat ease my body and quiet my mind. In the background, I could hear my husband in the living room, the low murmur of the television drifting through the house. Then, without warning, the Spirit stirred within me—gently at first, then with undeniable force—and I began to sing in tongues, letting the sound rise up like a prayer I didn't understand but deeply felt.

And then… something unexplainable happened.

From the other room, a woman's voice joined mine—not just singing, but harmonizing perfectly, note for note, spirit to spirit. My breath caught. It was as if Heaven had tuned us together in that sacred moment.

Grabbing a robe, heart racing, I rushed into the living room. There was a band called *Three O'Clock Session* performing live. The voice I had heard, the harmony that met mine—it was the singer's. Somehow, across airwaves and unseen realms, we had sung together. I still cannot tell you how it happened, only that it did—and that something holy moved through the music that night.

But wait, it gets even more incredible.

That night, sleep brought a vision: a massive white clock, glowing in a still, silent space. The clock read exactly three o'clock. The hands, strikingly gold, gleamed like sunlight caught in motion.

Then, the following night, I had another dream. Two towering oak trees appeared, their forms unmistakable despite being completely hidden. Every inch of their branches, every open space, was alive with red cardinals. Not a glimpse of sky, not a single leaf in view—it was just an endless sea of vibrant red wings.

Cardinals have always carried a special meaning, and in that moment, their presence felt divine. The trees stood strong, unseen yet known, cloaked in something holy.

An urgent conviction in my spirit drove me to see this man in person, no matter the cost, and I knew I had to go wherever he was. I checked Dr. Kevin Zadai's event page and found it led to Lostant, Illinois, so I called the number listed and spoke to the pastor, who confirmed Dr. Zadai would be coming that month. I immediately purchased a plane ticket and rented an Airbnb.

I would be visiting the River of Destiny Church to see him. The funny thing is, I thought I was going to Louisiana. I had no idea where Lostant even was. I didn't even care. The address of the Airbnb was One River Way, which I thought was pretty ironic. After landing and exiting the plane, I went straight to the rental car counter and picked up my keys. I was shocked when I saw a bright red convertible in the parking lot. It was just like the one in my dream.

Being stressed about having to drive two hours through a cornfield to get to my room, I drove directly to the venue, which turned out to be a school gymnasium. They had to rent this space to fit all the guests who had signed up. The excitement was thick, and the expectations were tangible. When I got there, the pastor greeted me at the school entrance. She told me I had to leave because it was too early to be there.

Not knowing where to go, I thought I would retrace my steps backward. Well, that didn't happen. I was lost out in the middle of a cornfield. To make matters worse, I completely lost my phone signal. Driving in circles, I could only imagine what the angels must have been saying to themselves. I came upon a tavern nestled in some woods. I was so happy and relieved. A group of drunks gave me directions back to the school! GOD! Group of Drunks! Now that's divine intervention! How ironic that I had been sober for over a decade.

This time a very sweet woman by the name of Kari Gold invited me to the front of the line. This afforded me the opportunity to be in the second row from the front. I will never forget Dr. Kevin Zadai's coming out and taking that stage by storm. He spoke in tongues for at least fifteen minutes straight. I wasn't used to this, but I chimed right in with everyone. As I looked up at the stage, there it was: a huge white clockface with gold numbers that read, "Three O'Clock Session." It was absolutely the same one I had seen in my dream the week prior. This man spoke with a wisdom and understanding that I had never experienced before. Savoring every word like a ribeye steak, the atmosphere became thick and holy. I knew in my "knower" why the Spirit led me here.

> *We can all draw close to Him with the veil removed from our faces. And with no veil we all become like mirrors who brightly reflect the glory of the Lord Jesus.*
>
> **—2 Corinthians 3:18 TPT**

During one intermission between sessions, I glanced down at the floor. There, as clear as day, I saw a river running right down the aisle in front of me. As I gazed down into the water in sheer amazement, the ripples diminished, and I began to see my reflection. But after looking closely for a few moments, I realized that it was not my reflection at all; I was looking right into the face of Jesus.

That first Friday evening, as I sat in my room, I looked out at the river. One cardinal after the other began landing in the yard. Covered in snow, these red birds started popping up everywhere. They were so enchanting. I suddenly began to feel a presence in that room. My spiritual senses were awakened and placed in overdrive. I don't know how others perceive the Spirit. All I knew was that there was something there in that room with me. I knew the atmosphere had changed. I knew, in the deepest part of my being, something or someone was there with me.

On the second day of that conference, I was en route to the venue again. It was icy cold, and it had snowed a lot. I had called my husband and wasn't paying attention to the road very well. The visibility was low to begin with because it was snowing. I looked up and saw a train track. I heard the train coming but I had no idea how far out it was. I decided to try and race through the track before it signaled me to stop. I was in a hurry and didn't want to wait. That train missed me by a hair, and I do mean by a hair. I caught hell from my husband, who was listening on the other end of the phone. Mercy and grace followed me once again. Praise be to God. Trains would become a common theme in my dream life years later.

So now it was the second session, and I was so excited, so expectant. If anyone ever tells you to lower your expectations, don't listen to that person. Expectation is a God-given source of spiritual power. Dr. Kevin Zadai looked right at me and said, "I break the spirit of poverty off you now! In the name of Jesus!" It was just like I had dreamed. Everything I had seen in my dreams the week prior was being played out right before my eyes. I was beginning to sense there was much more unraveling in the spirit realm.

Could the Holy Spirit have brought me to this conference because He had ordained these very moments?

That conference was epic and one I will remember forever. I met Tony Kemp for the first time. I saw people radically changed and healed right on the stage in front of me. One woman was glued to the floor for over twenty minutes as the Lord ministered healing to her brain. I found out later that she had had surgery in the past. That same woman turned out to be Dr. Kevin Zadai's camera operator. I have seen her at many of his events since then, and she is thriving. There is no limit to what God can do through a surrendered vessel.

Sunday, the last day of sessions, a young man came up to me and placed a ten-dollar bill in my hand. I asked him what it was for. "I want to be the first to sow into your ministry," he said. "I don't have a ministry," I explained, feeling bad about taking his money. He looked me in the eyes and said, "You will!"

Anxious to get home, I drove to the airport the next day. As I waited at the gate, I looked up and saw a wall completely covered in red cardinals. Cardinals lined the wall from top to bottom. It was a very clever way to display the state bird key-chains being sold. Again, there was another dream being played out in real time. Now I call them "signposts along the way." God has a beautiful way of letting us know we are exactly where we are supposed to be.

I arrived home, so excited to share with friends and family what had happened over the weekend. Immediately I perceived something was very different. The atmosphere around me had changed. I was beginning to see colors everywhere. They were coming out in pictures mostly. At night when my husband and I turned down the lights, we began to see those colors swirling all around us. Sometimes we could sense a fluttering, like a movement in the corners of our room.

The realm of the spirit had opened to me, and I had no clue what was happening. As Dr. Kevin Zadai would say, "I received my package." And perhaps a bit more.

By this point, I had been sober for sixteen years and was very open to the things of the Spirit. I had learned how to search myself, to forgive, and to love without conditions. I can only share my truth and experiences. God has opened my scrolls in my heart. I will do whatever it takes for me to stay on the path He prepared for me before I was even conceived in my mother's womb.

Previously, life had always been hit or miss. Dr. Zadai refers to this as "bumper car faith." We throw anything out there and hope we hit something. Then comes a time when you know you are hitting the mark. A level of maturity has been reached, and you begin walking in your God-given authority. The beauty in all of it is that I sought Him and I caught Him. What used to be a struggle was becoming an effortless one-on-one communication with the Holy Spirit.

I used to think only others who were more godly, more educated, could see spiritually. Gradually this ability began to erupt and seep out from my heart, and I started to see and feel through my spirit. What a revelation. First Chronicles 28:9 was becoming a reality!

If the Lord can search a man's heart and we are made in His image, then we also as sons of God can function in the same capacity. Some refer to this as cardiognosis. I was beginning to have a strong confidence in God's promises. I held onto hope despite all the curveballs being thrown at me. I began silencing that voice that once told me to "give up; this is too hard for you to handle."

Chapter 5

THE NIGHT WATCHMAN

In November 2019, the Lord began revealing to me the enemy's agenda' mostly in dreams and visions. One dream I clearly remember was set in a hospital. I was working on one of the higher levels. My six-year-old daughter had come out of one room. Her cheeks were red and flushed. I hurried her back into her room and had her wait there for me. In the next scene I am walking down the corridor of an airport. I saw a "Red Baron® Pizza" place coming up. I thought, *I'll go in and get a slice.*

When I walked up to the counter, I saw they had been shut down and were no longer serving. As I gazed down the hall, I could see that all the eateries had been shut down. I felt disappointed. I stepped away from the counter and saw a tall nurse in a freshly pressed white lab coat. I knew she was very accomplished and very professional. Intuitively, I just knew she was a top-notch nurse.

Then I'm back in the hospital, looking straight into a patient's room. I see a woman with yellowish skin. She had a tiara on her head, and her nails were long and painted a sparkly red color. Everyone who walked by her room was admiring her pretty nails, but she was so emaciated, the hospital had to make a special bed for her. It resembled a casket. I went back to look at her a second time, and there was a second woman lying in a casket-style bed as well alongside her. The two women were both hooked up to a single respirator. I suddenly realized I was in the critical care unit and that the hospital was filled beyond its capacity. The dream ended.

The Lord was showing me what was coming. The women were Asian, as evidenced by their long red nails and yellowish skin tone. There was one breathing machine to support two people in an overcrowded hospital. I found it very interesting that the restaurant was the "Red Baron." Red can symbolize war, sin, and death. Barren (the homophone for "baron") can symbolize a curse or spirit of death. It would only be a short time before Covid-19 would invade our nation. My daughter's cheeks were red, but she was still alive. This was an indication that children would be more likely to live through it, and high fevers would be the worst they would have to deal with.

I don't typically read the newspaper. I had taken a stack from my mother's home to line my bird's cages. As I looked down, I read, "New York City Hospitals Overcrowded, Patients forced to share one ventilator." Wow!

A few weeks later, I dreamed of two former presidents strolling along a path in front of the White House. Then the scene changed to a hospital ward. There were people in wheelchairs everywhere. A former first lady was pushing an elderly woman down the hallway, and several people got up out of their wheelchairs and fell dead. I saw a former president behind the nurse's station, sitting there with a smug look on his face. He smiled an evil smile, and I saw drops of blood come down from the corner of his mouth as he grinned devilishly. He then held up a blood-stained key. The key began to crumble. The Lord showed me who was behind the scenes of our country's up-and-coming attacks and attempts to depopulate our nation.

These dreams came in quick succession. It was one after the other. These dreams needed no interpretation. They were very clear and concise. As I began journaling and researching many of the messages I was receiving, I felt a stirring in my spirit to search out more Scriptures and to search for newspaper articles. The dots were slowly connecting. The Lord of angel armies was alerting me of things to come.

> *But when the truth-giving Spirit comes, he will unveil the reality of every truth within you. He won't speak on his own, but only what he hears from the Father, and he will reveal prophetically to you what is to come.*
>
> **—John 16:13 TPT**

At first, I didn't realize the significance of it all. When the God of the universe begins to reveal deep mysteries and forewarns of future events, it's something that shouldn't be ignored. I felt compelled to pray and intercede on behalf of the country, stepping into unfamiliar territory. There is power in numbers, though, and an inner urgency grew in me to connect with like-minded believers and agree in prayer. It became clear that only a handful of people could be trusted with my thoughts and conclusions, as most circles weren't receptive to them.

By the end of that month, I was so on fire for God, I could hardly contain it. My pastor had phoned my husband and asked that I curb my enthusiasm. I was so hurt. We had been leading the Wednesday night prayer meeting. My husband and I noticed that the pastor and his wife were putting the reins on us. We stayed there a few weeks longer. Then I had a dream. I saw the pastor's wife stomping on an altar that contained our scrolls.

The next night, I dreamed that Dr. Kevin Zadai was sitting at a desk, looking at me. He clearly stated, "You cannot compromise!" Together, Doug and I decided not to return to that church. It would have been easy to lose hope and feel alone, but all the teachings from Dr. Zadai explained how the remnant would be set apart. We began watching more online services and attended every conference that was within driving distance.

In December 2019 and into the spring of 2020, I began meeting regularly with a group of young people from Del Rio in a Zoom prayer group. We would read several Bible chapters and then have a discussion. This was such a blessing at first. I felt as though I had found my tribe. I was excited to meet with them and was really getting to know some of them on a deeper level. I had shared with the group many of my testimonies of how the Lord led me to the rooms of Alcoholics Anonymous.

When I realized some members of this group were extremely disturbed, I offered to pray with them on an individual basis. This was too early on in my understanding of how deliverance worked, so it really backfired on me. I began having nightmares. Some of them were so terrifying. I believe it was because of the soul ties that I had developed with some members of this group.

Later that year, I decided to stop meeting with them. I kept to myself once again, watching Sid Roth's programs or finding anything I could that had to do with the realm of the spirit. I ordered a slew of books on the prophetic from authors such as James Goll and John Eckhardt. I had been following Dr. Kevin Zadai on YouTube and had already purchased some of his books and even began taking his course "Heavenly Visitation."

I truly believe that the Lord had a divine plan to connect me with this ex-flight attendant turned preacher. Sometimes, if I had a question or a concern, Dr. Kevin Zadai would come to me in a dream and show me the answer or give me some advice on what to do.

On February 25, 2020, my dream journal entry was this: *"I was writing down Scriptures in a book. I was telling someone my truths were 'already written'; therefore, they override all the lies."* This was so significant because I would soon learn Psalm 139:16 (TPT) reads: "You saw who you created me to be before I became me! Before I'd ever seen the light of day, the number of days you planned for me were already recorded in your book." This dream confirmed that very Scripture!

One day in March, I sat up in my bed during the wee hours of the morning. I looked over toward the stairway and saw a purple crucifix floating in midair. It was spinning and turning. Right beside it was a huge purple butterfly. I could mostly see the outline of the butterfly, but it was very large, and its wings were flapping. I remember this so clearly, as if it was yesterday.

Proverbs 25:2 says that "it is the glory of God to conceal a matter, but the glory of kings is to search out a matter." Purple, as described in Barbie Breathitt's *A-Z Dream Symbology Dictionary*, "represents God our eternal King; authority; royalty; intercession; and creativity.[3]" Butterfly means change and transformation into freedom. Butterflies have two eyes that see in the natural and in ultraviolet realms.

> *Therefore, if anyone is in Christ, he is a new creation; old things have passed away; behold, all things have become new.*
>
> **—2 Corinthians 5:17**

The Lord has a beautiful way of sharing His heart with those who will listen.

3. Barbie Breathitt, *A-Z Dream Symbology Dictionary,* s.v., "purple" (self-published, 2015).

On August 24, 2020, I had my "Trump" dream. I dreamed that the FBI was trying to catch the "redhead." The FBI was banging on my front door. I was doing everything I could to stop them from bursting in. When I turned back and faced the living room, I saw a woman with red hair hiding under the couch.

Quickly my attention was brought to an enormous television set sitting in the middle of the living room floor. Talk about a play on words: "tell-a-vision." I saw President Trump speaking to me from this television, except his head was real; it was not a broadcast. He looked right at me and stated, "I am your president."

I saw the truth. I felt the scandalous nature behind this vision. All the prayers in the world didn't stop what happened. I know God is not the author of this chaos and assault on our freedom. I do believe He allows things to happen because He knows that a depraved generation will soon be on their knees, searching for His mercy like never before. I believe we are there now. The world will soon come to know the entire truth. President Trump had been stolen from. Our nation had been stolen from. This prophetic insight astounded me. I continued to watch closely as I realized the Lord was revealing His perfect will versus His permissive will.

From the year 2019 until early 2022, I saw more supernatural events than I ever thought possible. Faculty members were lining up at the clinic door, asking me to pray for their family members. The staff brought unruly students to me when they were acting out. The love of God was so strong in that space, these students would just drop to their knees and begin to weep.

Speaking of depraved generations, things had gotten so intensely weird at school. Kids were being arrested every other day. Handguns were being confiscated. Teens were overdosing at an alarming rate. Something in the atmosphere had changed, and it wasn't good. I even saw our attendance clerk run down by a speeding vehicle at eight o'clock in the morning.

Being a school nurse for 1,700 kids was overwhelming at times. I knew, spiritually, when a child came in with a curse versus a mild infirmity. After that first time seeing Dr. Kevin Zadai and receiving my "package," I had angels encamped all around the clinic. I began sensing and feeling them like never before. My eyes had opened up in the spirit. I would see rainbows everywhere. They were in the clinic. They were in my car and in my home. They followed me outside. When I would turn my lights out at night, I could see the movement of color in the corners of our bedroom. It was as if Heaven had invaded my space. The most exciting part of all this was that the children at school began getting instantly healed when they came to see me. Sometimes I would sing to them. Other times the Lord would have me lay hands on them. There were a few times students would just come through the door and begin weeping uncontrollably. I know the Healer was there.

> *God is our refuge and strength, an ever-present help in trouble.*
>
> **—Psalm 46:1 NIV**

Well, He was certainly there in that clinic because I had no power to heal or to restore anyone.

My encounters with one young lady really stuck out to me. She was brought down to me in her wheelchair twice a day for a meal that I administered through her gastric feeding tube. She would smile and was only able to repeat the words that were said to her. This is a strange disorder known as echolalia. I would always greet her with a smile and a song. I would put on some worship music and hold her hand and sing to her. She would come to expect this and show her displeasure with a frown if I didn't play songs for her. I began asking her questions and engaging with her more frequently.

I know she was able to discern the angels encamped around the room. It had only been a few weeks of our time together before I realized she was forming new words and answering questions rather than just repeating what was being said to her. She began singing along with the music. Her instructional assistant could hardly believe it. She would smile from ear to ear. Dancing and leaping around in her chair became her new norm. The power that raised Jesus from the dead was moving on her.

> *The Lord your God is with you, the Mighty Warrior who saves. He will take great delight in you; in his love he will no longer rebuke you, but will rejoice over you with singing.*
>
> **—Zephaniah 3:17 NIV**

I was beginning to realize that my weapon was a melody.

God was undoubtedly doing a new thing in my life. This fire was unquenchable. I sought for more, and He obliged me. There were a few times I got off track because I stumbled upon some new age speakers, but through His love and guidance, I quickly got back on course. There is a very present form of deception that has infiltrated the church and some ministers.

The Spirit has been teaching my family to recognize the truth. If there has ever been a need for discernment, that time is now. Separating the truth from the false was something I began doing as part of my inner healing when I got sober in 2003. I see now why the Lord had me go through the avenues He chose. I am so grateful for the Holy Spirit's wisdom and guidance. I understand now that discernment is the beginning of spiritual sight. I began seeing through the eyes of faith. Now faith was becoming a living, moving deluge of healing and restoration like I had never before experienced. My partnership with the Lord had unlocked a movement in that clinic that I never dreamed was even possible. The God in me had created a community of healing and a safe place for the students and staff to come for emotional and physical healing.

Chapter 6

IT'S A FAMILY AFFAIR

I am the Alpha and the Omega, the First and the Last, the Beginning and the End.

—Revelation 22:13 NIV

On my way to work one morning, as I was driving up an incline on a beautiful road just outside of San Antonio, my attention was brought to a bright shimmering light off in the distance. Thank goodness there was no one behind me because I started slowing down to get a better look at what I was seeing. There was a huge shape, a form, floating down out of the sky toward my windshield. It was very bright, and it was beckoning me. I stared at this thing for several moments, just in awe. I gazed at my clock, and it read 7:23. I didn't want to hold up traffic, so I kept driving.

As soon as I arrived at work, I hopped onto my computer to look into the symbol. Sure enough, it was the alpha symbol, bright as could be and coming straight for me.

Now this was exciting, but what was even more exciting was that my husband had been driving my daughter to school that same morning, and they both saw the omega symbol out on top of a hilltop. I asked him, "Honey! What time was it?" He replied, "It was 7:27 am because I looked at my clock on the dashboard." When I realized what we were both seeing, I was in shock.

The Lord was showing us something very profound.

> *And I heard a loud voice from heaven saying, "Behold, the tabernacle of God is with men, and He will dwell with them, and they shall be His people. God Himself will be with them and be their God. And God will wipe away every tear from their eyes; there shall be no more death, nor sorrow, nor crying. There shall be no more pain, for the former things have passed away." Then He who sat on the throne said, "Behold, I make all things new." And He said to me, "Write, for these words are true and faithful." And He said to me, "It is done! I am the Alpha and the Omega, the Beginning and the End. I will give of the fountain of the water of life freely to him who thirsts. He who overcomes shall inherit all things, and I will be his God, and he shall be My son."*
>
> **—Revelation 21:3–7**

The timing was prophetic. It lines up perfectly with this portion of Scripture. Since we had made Him our all in all, our everything, He showed us our inheritance. This was a beautiful way the Lord spoke to us as a family. It could not be denied. My husband was sure this is what he and Kendall had seen that morning. "And he shall be My son" was a profound message for my husband. If he ever thought that God hadn't included him in all of His plans, that misconception was blown completely out of the water. Doug began experiencing powerful encounters with the Holy Spirit too numerous to mention. This encounter fueled a fire in my husband that I doubt he even knew was lit to begin with.

This was a day that marked our family forever.

Autumn has always held a special place in my heart. For my family, it's a season wrapped in warmth and gratitude, when familiar childhood favorite movies return to our screens and remind us of simpler days. One of those has always been *Willy Wonka and the Chocolate Factory* (1971). God only knows why, but that story has always stirred something deep within me.

It was late November when I had another dream encounter. In the dream, my husband and I were invited into Willy Wonka's office. With a sense of peace, I handed him my piece of the Everlasting Gobstopper. The moment I did, the scene changed.

Suddenly, my husband and I were in that great glass elevator, rising high above the earth—higher and higher—until we reached what felt like the edge of Heaven's atmosphere. Looking out through the glass, I saw a vast expanse of brilliant white, glistening as if made of pure diamonds. It was breathtaking. I turned to my husband, filled with awe and wonder at the beauty before us. Then the dream gently ended.

It took years for me to understand what the Lord was showing us. Now I know that the Holy Spirit was speaking. The message was simple yet profound: *God trusts us.* We had been faithful stewards over what He had placed in our hands. The "grand prize" was not earthly reward, but divine affirmation—a reminder that when we walk in obedience and integrity, Heaven takes notice. Diving even deeper, when I read the book of Ezekiel and came across the vision of the wheel within a wheel, I was absolutely captivated! This incredible, otherworldly creature—covered in eyes all around—moved effortlessly in every direction, up and down, back and forth, just like the glass elevator!

After my first adventure in Illinois seeing Dr. Kevin Zadai and becoming completely set on fire, my hunger and thirst for more became insatiable. Dr. Kevin invited everyone to take something from the book table, so I took one of everything. I later realized that I had overdone it. I wrote a check to his ministry for the full amount for all the CDs I had taken and mailed it off to them. God in His mercy still blessed me because I made a living amends. I became completely saturated with the Word of God and Dr. Kevin's teachings that were on those CDs. I had not truly understood what the term *impartation* meant until I experienced it firsthand.

Later that week, I had an open vision. Among trees in a forest, I was wearing a wedding gown. Tilting my head down, I noticed I was wearing a beautiful sheer veil. A hand reached over and pulled the veil away from my face. I looked up and smiled, then the vision ended.

That evening, my five-year-old daughter fell asleep in our bed. During the night, I had what felt like a dream. I got up and tried looking out the window, but there was a curtain. I could vaguely see people walking by. Someone was riding a bicycle. I remember trying to lift the curtain to see. Suddenly, my daughter sat up in bed and said, "I can see right through it, Mommy! Put the curtain down." This was still all part of the dream. Or was it? We never actually woke up. My daughter did not remember waking up during the night. Was this a dream? I know my daughter sat up and spoke to me. We had met in the realm of the spirit. This heart-to-heart encounter with my daughter helped me to realize that supernatural life is for everyone. In fact, it comes easier through the eyes of a child.

I believe there is a veil that overlays our hearts. It can prevent us from seeing and hearing God. This veil also separates us from giving and receiving love. Once that veil is removed, we are free to see and hear the way God originally intended. The Lord was comparing me to my five-year-old, who was full of trust and pure love. She delighted in simple things. She saw through eyes of wonder. This was a wake-up call for me to become more like a child—not childish, just childlike in my faith. What a simple but profound revelation.

Speaking of children in my life, I felt so defeated for so many years because my stepchildren just didn't seem to accept me. They were two and five years old when I married their father. When I learned how to pray, things began to get easier, and I received hope. One year, my husband and I drove to a Warrior Notes conference in Illinois. While I was there, I had an open vision. I saw my stepson sitting in the middle of a wheat field. He was smiling so big and was holding a piece of wheat between his teeth. The sun was shining upon him so brightly. His older sister was walking toward him. This vision gave me so much hope. I knew beyond a shadow of a doubt that God was working on their hearts behind the scenes. What once seemed like such a heavy burden to carry soon became much lighter. As I began to implement the prayer strategies of a warrior, as Dr. Kevin teaches, I began seeing results in our family's lives. Words like *counsel, altar, holiness,* and *covenant* have become household words in our home.

In less than one year from the time I had that open vision, my stepson gave his life to Yeshua. We had brought both of our little ones to a conference in Conroe, Texas. Connor answered the call Dr. Kevin made for anyone wanting to give his or her life to Christ. Connor and my daughter were eight years old when Dr. Kevin prayed for them and our family. Since that time, something has greatly changed. Many things have unfolded. My stepson talks about Jesus quite frequently. He has faith today and experiences our home as a safe haven.

Recently we were driving down a highway close to our home. We had set out to set up a deer feeder on a property that my husband began hunting on. We were all very excited about the trip. The deer feeder was tied to the back of my husband's pickup truck. As we were driving, my husband saw in the rearview mirror that the lid to the deer feeder had blown off. We spent twenty minutes driving up and down the highway searching for that lid. We combed the area between the grass and the guardrails several times. Eventually my husband gave up, and we began driving out of the area.

I heard Connor in the back ask, "Jesus, will You just drop my dad's lid out of the sky for us, please?" My husband and I were stunned when the lid fell out of the sky and landed on the side of the road, and he spotted it. There are no limits to what the Spirit of God can do.

If there is one thing I know, it is that God hears the prayers of His children. We live in a time where the innocence of our children is trying to be stolen right out from underneath us. Everything we see now on television and on social media is man celebrating his own achievements. Idols are being erected at every turn. Idols can be defined as anything we set our attention on before God. This includes social media, shopping, relationships, sex, food, and anything that tickles our ears. It has been a challenge trying to rear our children in the ways of God so that, when they are older, they will not depart from them (see Proverbs 22:6).

Through my studies at Warrior Notes School of Ministry, I was learning more about supernatural provision. Jesus's bag was always being handed out. The supply never ran dry, even with Judas's grubby little mitts getting in there. During this time, I would go to this gas station on the way to work. The pump would ask me every time, "Would you like the discount?" So, I would respond with an affirmative "Yes!" I didn't belong to any special club or have a credit card for this gas station. Somehow, I was given this supernatural blessing, which brought my gas total to about fifteen dollars for a full tank. This happened every time I went to fill up for two straight years. When I heard Dr. Zadai explaining how Jesus's bag never ran out, I was quickened in my spirit and knew exactly what the Lord had been doing for those two years.

Chapter 7

A SACRED SANCTIFICATION

Walking in the whisper of Moses…

How did I get here?

It was winter of 2019 when I had a dream I was climbing a mountain, wearing a pair of brown Roman sandals and a brown tunic. Suddenly, I came across a large mound of rocks. As I walked around this wall of stones, there were two stone tablets lying on the ground. Quickly scooping them up, I proceeded to carry them both until I got to the highest point of the mountain. As I turned to look down, I saw that both stone tablets had turned to flesh, with a peach-colored skin tone, and then the dream ended.

> *I will give you a new heart and put a new spirit in you; I will remove from you your heart of stone and give you a heart of flesh.*
>
> **—Ezekiel 36:26 NIV**

This dream encounter was meaningful. The Lord Himself was letting me know that I was a letter from Christ, not written with ink, but with the Spirit of the Living God (see 2 Corinthians 3:3). This symbolized an inner transformation rather than the external law-keeping that religion had taught me. The deeper contemplation of the tunic revealed a sacred symbol of the church's unity; it was seamless and whole, woven by divine hands into one living garment of faith.

Experiences just like this one began occurring on a regular basis. I had no idea that this was one of the ways God was showing me that my soul was lining up with my spirit—one integrated triune being, just like my Father. We were created in His image. The more I saw, the more I hungered for more. I decided to go see Dr. Kevin Zadai again, this time in Peru, Illinois, and invited my girlfriend, Carol, to go along.

One week before we left San Antonio for the conference in Illinois, I had a dream. I saw a billboard on the side of the road that read "Chuck S." in large letters, twice. I knew a Chuck S. in real life. He had just agreed to pray for me about something a few weeks prior. On our drive to Illinois, we drove right past that same exact billboard from my dream. I just knew that it was one of those signposts along the way. It was another double portion blessing. I was exactly where I was supposed to be at that very moment.

This trip to Illinois was especially exciting because apostle Tony Kemp and Dean Braxton were going to be at the conference. I knew Tony from our last encounter, but I had never heard about Dean Braxton. Apparently, Dean had been clinically dead for an hour and forty-five minutes. He met Jesus and the Father, much like Dr. Zadai, but his experience was completely different.

I felt truly blessed to attend this session and hear his testimony. As Carol and I were sitting in the lobby of our hotel, Tony Kemp walked in and sat down in a big easy chair by the fireplace. I asked, "Tony! How have you been?" Out of the goodness of his heart and most likely the direction of the Holy Spirit, he ministered to my girlfriend and me. We sat there for two hours soaking it all in. What a huge blessing that was. I learned so much about deliverance because he brought my friend through it right in front of me. What an exciting start to our weekend.

I told Tony Kemp about a dream I had where a white cloud, kind of like the one in the movie *Trolls* (2016), had been popping up everywhere. It would rest on my shoulder, and then it would jump onto my head. It seemed to have a non-distinct face. I would look on the floor, and it was following me. It was kind of comical. I looked up at Tony, and he was grinning. Then he stated, "You really love Jesus!" Indeed I do.

> *By day the* Lord *went ahead of them in a pillar of cloud to guide them on their way and by night in a pillar of*

fire to give them light, so that they could travel by day or night.

—Exodus 13:21 NIV

Sometimes things are so clear we can't even see them when they are right in front of us. When I woke up the next morning, I heard a song in my spirit. It was an oldie called "You Ain't Seen Nothing Yet" by Bachman-Turner Overdrive from 1974. I was about to get a supernatural gift from God I desperately needed.

As I mentioned earlier, my younger brother overdosed in 2018. Although I hoped he had entered Heaven, I had no way of being sure. That all ended after meeting Dean Braxton. He was giving us a play by play of what it was like to be at the throne worshiping with all the saints. His testimony was so on fire. You could see fire coming out of this man's eyes.

When Dean was finished speaking that day, I approached him and asked him if people who were on drugs could still make it to Heaven. I explained to him the dream I had where my brother came up from behind me and squeezed me so tightly, I could feel it in the natural. He showed me his glorified body. He wore a white sweatsuit and unzipped it as if he was unzipping his soul. An immense white light poured right out of him.

Dean immediately stopped me in my tracks. "When people go to hell, you don't see them again. They are down there and it's seared. The fact that you saw your brother in his glorified body is a sure sign he made it through that gate." He said it with such conviction.

I was so relieved. The Father had sent this precious soul to give me closure around my brother's passing. I have been at peace about it ever since. Do I miss my brother? You bet I do. But I also have this blessed assurance.

> *But our citizenship is in heaven, and from it we await a Savior, the Lord Jesus Christ, who will transform our lowly body to be like his glorious body, by the power that enables him even to subject all things to himself.*
>
> **—Philippians 3:20–21 ESV**

That encounter with Dean Braxton was life-changing and life-giving. I had received the gift of closure and peace. Where the wind in my sails had blown out, the Lord managed to fill me back up. I returned home after that weekend with more hope and more zeal than ever before.

Being under the corporate anointing had its advantages. As I was exposed to more of the Holy Spirit in large group settings, things began to get clearer not only in my understanding, but in the spirit as well. When like-minded people gather in one accord and the Lord is present to heal, all sorts of miraculous events can occur. Sometimes all it takes is a spoken word to see results manifest in the natural realm. When the spirit is stirred up, like the pool of Bethesda, you can be sure there will be a manifestation of healing and deliverance.

God began to root out all my old ideas and beliefs, replacing them with His realities, His truths. All it took was my cooperation and full surrender. For those who think that the sanctification process is quick and painless, think again. It is not an overnight process, and we are never really done building character. I would like to think the Lord started pouring out to me in dreams and in visions because I am special. What's more likely is that He couldn't get my attention because I was not fully yielded when I was awake.

Learning to take quiet time with my Father in order to hear what the Holy Spirit is saying is what changed my capacity to yield and understand. God can do whatever He wants whenever He wants, but we can be so much more effective in this life if we make Him our number one priority and slow down long enough to hear what is on His heart.

One of my favorite dreams was so short but so powerful. I had already begun taking multiple courses from the Warrior Notes School of Ministry. In this dream I was standing in front of a judge in a courtroom. I looked up to face the judge head-on and saw this huge black gavel come slamming down on the bench. I knew I had won. The victory was mine. Then the dream ended.

In his message, "How Your Spirit Is Wired to Heaven's Power and Provision," Dr. Kevin Zadai says, "When the gavel comes down, you are in the throne room of Heaven."[4]

---

4. Kevin Zadai, "How Your Spirit Is Wired to Heaven's Power and Provision," 2025 Spirit School & One Night Meetings, May 15, 2025, https://www.youtube.com/watch?v=3kWFmadz2I0.

So now the case is closed. There remains no accusing voice of condemnation against those who are joined in life-union with Jesus, the Anointed One.

—Romans 8:1 TPT

Warrior justice was not just a message Dr. Zadai preached; it was a divine summons that echoed through every conference like a trumpet blast from Heaven. I had heard those Scriptures many times before, but until that moment, they felt distant, like they belonged to someone else more worthy. Shame, guilt, and self-condemnation had quietly built walls around me, keeping me confined in a place far smaller than the destiny God had prepared.

But then came the dream—holy, unmistakable, and liberating. It shattered the chains I didn't even know still bound me. In that sacred moment, I was set free—not just emotionally, but also spiritually. I released the past like shedding a burial cloth and leaped into the now, into the fullness of who I was created to be.

What a holy gift it is to finally live unbound.

The Lord is my shepherd; I shall not want. He makes me lie down in green pastures; He leads me beside the still waters. He restores my soul....

—Psalm 23:1–3

One morning, during winter that same year, I was driving to work and began listening to one of Kevin's audio CDs titled

"Supernatural Displacement." I was about a third through it when I glanced over to the right side of the road. All the grass in that area had died and was brown because it was already cold and all the leaves had begun turning.

Suddenly, the entire landscape turned bright green. It was the brightest green I had ever seen. What I had been listening to on the CD had manifested right before my eyes. I even looked away and took a double take. Sure enough, the countryside was all lit up in the most radiant green color. This really floored me. I could only imagine what Heaven was like.

It was clear to see that my spiritual eyes had opened. But was it clear? Clear as mud, maybe. No matter how many times these manifestations occur, we just can't believe how awesome our God is. I began to live in eager expectation of what God was going to do next. I think back now on all the hours I spent sitting quietly, just hoping to get a glimpse or take a flier into the realm of the spirit.

Now it was as if a floodgate had opened, and the river of life was being poured out on me. Every day became an adventure. I soon realized that an impartation could be received if I was open-minded and willing to yield. I spent countless hours, days, and years watching all the generals of the faith, present and past, hoping to absorb their pearls of wisdom. There was an absolute truth that trumped reality as I knew it. Finally, this was becoming my new normal.

My entire family was becoming engulfed in a new magnificent world of God's normal. The Spirit's presence could be seen and felt throughout every inch of our home. There were days when I could hardly contain myself. Kendall, my youngest daughter, was also having open visions and more descriptive dreams. We knew she was marked. She would dive into all the spiritual material presented to her. Attending a private Christian school in the Hill Country was a blessing because it fostered a bigger desire in her to seek her own truth.

It was late December that same year, and one beautiful evening in the Hill Country, my family and I were invited to our daughter Kendall's Christmas play at the White Rock Church. Funny thing about those white rocks—they seem to have become a theme in my life. My family was sitting in one of the pews up front, waiting for the play to begin. My husband leaned over to tell me something his ex-wife had said about me earlier that day. I can't recall his exact words, but I can tell you it was neither kind nor loving. As I looked up toward him, I saw a flaming arrow come shooting straight at me in slow motion. It stopped about three inches from my chest, and I saw it crumble to the ground. My eyes had opened in the spirit realm, and I was given the opportunity to see my shield in action.

> *"No weapon formed against you shall prosper, and every tongue which rises against you in judgment you shall condemn. This is the heritage of the servants of the Lord, and their righteousness is from Me," says the Lord.*

—Isaiah 54:17

In another dream, we were driving to Conroe, Texas, to see Dr. Kevin Zadai. I asked my husband to pull over so I could use the restroom. My husband and I walked up a path leading to the door of the facility. There was a large gray trash can in front of the door. For me to get in, my husband had to lift it up and move it aside. After he did, we both looked down to see a very large, white, flat rock. Written in red flower petals were the words "Pretty Flower."

The scene changed, and then there was a man pulling food out of the back of his hatchback vehicle. We walked over to see what the commotion was about. We were handed a huge stack of ham steaks. We walked away astounded with our arms full of meat.

> *He who has an ear, let him hear what the Spirit says to the churches. To him who overcomes I will give some of the hidden manna to eat. And I will give him a white stone, and on the stone a new name written which no one knows except him who receives it.*
>
> **—Revelation 2:17**

The idea of a new name on the white rock really stood out for me. In the days to come, I was literally bombarded with Scriptures containing images of flowers. They were coming to me in droves. Facebook especially was where I saw the most. It was as if each message was tailored for me. This was also a time when Dr. Zadai's teachings were getting more intense. I was really feasting on the meat of the Word and so grateful that his explanations of the Scriptures went so deep beneath the surface. When Dr. Kevin Zadai publishes a book, you had better believe it is going to have its fair share of Scripture.

Three years later, I received another layer of the interpretation of that dream. God was showing me the stakes were high. If the body of Christ doesn't take its rightful position, then there could be significant consequences that affect generations to come. I was quick to downplay this beautiful encounter that God had given me. I thought my new name should have been "Victorious Warrior" or "Lion of Judah."

After reflecting on it for a few months, something inside of me clicked. Jesus sees His bride like a flower in bloom. A negative self-image was something I struggled with most of my life, but if this was the Lord's view of me, who was I to disagree? I was just so overwhelmed to have been given my new name. A few weeks after this, I was at an actual conference of Dr. Kevin's and was handed a flat stone by one of the children, and the stone read "courage." This really warmed my heart, and I knew the Lord had ordained that moment.

Eventually, later in the summer of 2025, the Warrior Notes team began tailgate lunches during its mentorship sessions. Wouldn't you know, I was handed a ham sandwich! Just like the dream where they handed us ham steaks.

My dreams began to increase in frequency and duration. I woke up one morning with "Joshua 1:8" floating right in front of my face and resting on my chest. The letters and numbers were an amber color and seemed to be like burning bronze. I was wide awake.

> *This Book of the Law shall not depart from your mouth, but you shall meditate in it day and night, that you may observe to do. . . .*
>
> **—Joshua 1:8**

I received direct marching orders from the King of Kings! If one is to flow in revelation knowledge, one had better know his or her Bible.

Chapter 8

FINDING REFINEMENT THROUGH FIRE

Have you ever felt like your dream life was off the charts? That was my world around the end of the 2021 school year. One of the major ways the Lord speaks to me is through my dreams. When He especially wants to get something across to me, I become very sleepy, and it's almost unbearable to stay awake. I know if I fall asleep, God will speak to me in my dreams.

One afternoon I was sitting in the clinic around 3:00 pm and became very sleepy, so I told my assistant I was just going to lie down for a few minutes. Maria was a very close friend of mine, and we had grown to love each other over the years we worked together. She would always say the rosary every day at 3:00 pm.

Maria told me, "Go lie down and pull the curtain. I'll take any kids that come in."

I went back and lay down and immediately started dreaming. In the dream, my husband and I were kneeling on top of an infinity sign that was on the floor. We were engulfed in blue and white flames. I remember looking to the side of the room and seeing what looked like an altar. There were black stones going from the floor up to the top of this piece of furniture. Some stones were small, and some were larger. The fire consumed everything. My husband and I both walked toward the altar. I woke up, sweating profusely and thinking that I was on fire. I shouted, "I'm on fire! I'm on fire!" and Maria came running into the room. She had to calm me down and assure me there was no fire.

Having no grid for a dream of this nature, I was disturbed at first. This was before I truly understood the concept of holy fire, and I realized the Lord was refining my husband and me. Barbie Breathitt's *A-Z Dream Symbology Dictionary* links altars to the "discipline of prayer being needed: laying down one's life; a memorial of life events; and access to God's heart.[5]" Fire was the presence of God. I knew from my reading and studying that the fire burns away the wood, hay, and stubble. No doubt our stones still have some edges that need smoothing. I was very relieved that my husband was there in the dream with me.

---

5. Barbie Breathitt, *A-Z Dream Symbology Dictionary,* s.v., "altar" (self-published, 2015).

For me, this meant my husband and I would be refined in the fire together, having memorial stones to share with others when we shared our testimonies. God spared us both from the flames of hell. We are both so grateful to have been set apart for the glory of God.

When I recollect this dream, I see myself there once again. Infinity is a mathematical symbol that represents something that is endless, unlimited, or without bounds. Once again, the Lord reminds me that when we stand on Him, we have access to it all.

I shared this dream with my husband. I wanted him to know how intense it was and how God has His eye on him also.

On the opposite spectrum, there is water. I had many dreams of wading through water—of water pouring through windows, waterfalls, dams breaking, and so forth. But this one dream stood out to me. I had it around the same time I had the fire dream in the clinic. I clearly recall a beautiful, rather large wooden bowl. It was made of acacia wood. Its base was a spindle, and it had been tipped over. The water had begun pouring out. It wasn't a trickle; a large amount of fresh, clean, crystal-like water came roaring out of this bowl. It was supernatural. Then I woke up.

> *But I will rejoice even if my life is poured out like a liquid offering to God over your sacrificial and surrendered lives of faith.*
>
> **—Philippians 2:17 TPT**

When I tell these dream accounts to others, they are more than dreams. A lingering substance is attached to them. I also remind Jesus of the dreams. He is not a man that He should lie; He will not go back on His Word (see Numbers 23:19). So, I mix it with faith. I get excited for the future because I know it's all in there. We call those things that are not as though they were (see Romans 4:17). I know from personal experience that we can change outcomes with prayer, fasting, believing, decreeing, and declaring. My favorite virtue is hope. I learned the acronym for hope, which is "Hearing Other People's Experiences." Now the Scripture makes sense:

> *And they overcame him by the blood of the Lamb, and by the word of their testimony; and they loved not their lives unto the death.*
>
> **—Revelation 12:11 KJV**

I was still working as a school nurse when Covid-19 swept the nation. Many people were getting sick, and many were dying. Although mask mandates were very strict in some states, my family and I refused to wear them. We would attend Dr. Zadai's conferences, and he would never have a mask on. We knew we were safe and protected in that environment. My friend and assistant Maria had retired at the end of 2020. Things were about to change drastically at work.

On Sunday, March 20, 2021, I had a vivid and unforgettable dream. I was stepping out of my car and walking toward my house. When I was halfway to the door, I looked up—and there stood Jesus.

He was on a ladder before my door, smearing His blood upon the doorposts with His own hands. He wore the garments of His suffering—no shirt, no shoes—just the marks of His love. As I approached, He turned and looked at me over His shoulder, and He smiled. I could see the sweat upon His face as the sunlight shone on Him.

That moment pierced my heart. The Lord of all creation knows my name, my home, my very steps. His blood covers me completely. I don't know how He could have made that truth any clearer.

It was a holy reminder of His covenant love and protection—a personal assurance that His blood was poured out for me. It was a blessing beyond words.

> *When the Lord goes through the land to strike down the Egyptians; he will see the blood on the top and sides of the doorframe and will pass over that doorway, and he will not permit the destroyer to enter your houses and strike you down.*
>
> **—Exodus 12:23 NIV**

Although the Lord was assuring me that I was covered by His blood, He never came out and said, "Kimberly, you're not ever going to get sick again." In fact, my entire immediate family all got a severe case of Covid-19 after traveling to Murfreesboro,

Tennessee, to visit the evangelical pastor Jeff Jansen, who was leading Global Fire Ministries. It was a wonderful conference, but my husband and I seemed to be knocking at death's door. It took months for us to recover fully.

This is why, now, I really heed Dr. Zadai's advice to be "sent" rather than "went." The apostle Paul says, "It seemed good to the Holy Spirit and to us..." Acts 15:28 NIV. This was Paul's inner witness letting him know a thing was right. I had not yet gotten into the habit of seeking the Holy Spirit on these sorts of matters. Thus, the enemy had found an open door for sickness to land. Since that time, I have learned that it really is God's will for us to prosper.

> *Beloved, I pray that you may prosper in all things and be in health, just as your soul prospers.*
>
> **—3 John 1:2**

The belief of many is that God gives them sickness to try and test them. By understanding God and His ways, I have come to know that God's will is never for anyone to be sick. It is never His will for anyone to perish. If we are not anchored in this truth, we will never be able to go forward with His plans for us. How can we blame God and love Him too? That makes no sense.

The next few months got weird. A friend from AA had called for moral support. That's one thing that I love about the AA program: Any time I was feeling down or felt like I needed advice, I could always call someone in the program. (AA's Responsibility

Statement says, "I am responsible, when anyone, anywhere reaches out for help, I want the hand of AA always to be there. And for that: I am responsible."[6]) So, this person is on the other end of the line, and I know she's upset because her husband decided to leave her earlier that week. Her hair had been falling out for weeks in big clumps.

Suddenly, we were off on a tangent and started talking about politics, which is something the members of AA are encouraged not to do. In meetings, we don't talk about politics, nor do we talk about religion. She started a rant about her liberal views and why she was voting for Joe Biden for president.

As I began to share my views on who I supported and the biblical principles I believed to back up my choices, I felt as if I had been pelted in the face with a handful of BB pellets. They came right through the receiver and hit me smack in the face. She wanted to argue with me about my choices. The Holy Spirit said, "Hang up! You are talking to a goat." Soon after this occurrence, I watched a conference online where Dr. Zadai explained to the audience how the seed of the Word will come back and smack him in the face if it is not received.

I knew then exactly what he was referring to. Let me assure you, it did not feel good. It felt awful—not so much physically, but spiritually. I was grieved as the Holy Spirit was grieved.

This experience shook me to my very core—it was as if the foundations of my being trembled beneath me! I knew deep

6. Alcoholics Anonymous, website, accessed December 3, 2025, https://www.aa.org/participating-in-aa.

within that God created me for one purpose: to serve Him and His people. Yet, feeling like an outsider in recovery meetings only deepened the ache inside. *How,* I wondered, *could I pour out all that had been so graciously poured into me?* These questions raced through my mind like a mighty river, unrelenting and loud.

I began spending a lot more time in prayer and a lot less time going to AA meetings. They were good for a large season of my life, but how can I go sit next to someone who describes their God as a tree or a bird? I don't avoid nonbelievers, but as Amos 3:3 says, can two walk together unless they agree?

The Lord began putting people on my heart frequently. When He did, I would just pray that God's will be done in their life. When there was someone who really needed urgent prayer, He would show me specifically what to pray about. More than anything, I personally felt a call, a tug in my spirit, to pray for the governments around the world. I jumped at any chance I could to gather with the remnant to intercede on America's behalf.

Then suddenly—like the dawn bursting forth after a long night—the answer came rushing in! It was as though the heavens opened and the Lord Himself began to pour revelation into my spirit faster than I could receive it. I was called to pray—for people.

Chapter 9

FULL CIRCLE FAITH

One evening while soaking in a hot bath, asking the Lord to speak to my heart, suddenly, the weight of silence pressed down on me as I gazed into a burning candle, until I declared, "I won't leave this bathroom until I hear from You."

Little did I know that this simple declaration would open the door to a breathtaking vision that would leave me awe-struck—and change everything I thought I knew about divine encounters.

I waited and waited. I got nothing. I could hear my husband watching the news from the other room. I sat there disgusted, yet my heart told me not to give up. This time when I closed my eyes, I saw a paintbrush with bright yellow paint on it. It began sweeping counterclockwise in a circle until all I could see was a bright yellow sun. I was so delighted and shocked, I tried not to move or blink. As the sun faded away, I realized I was in a small cave, looking out into the sky. Over to my left was a small cloud about the size of a man's fist. That cloud gradually came into focus, becoming heavy, deep, and profound—and I sensed that it brimmed with purpose, ready to release its life-giving rain. Utterly amazed, I noticed the clouds to my right began moving. Suddenly, I saw the upper right quadrant of a man's face. I homed in on His great big blue eye. It was peering down at me. It saw me. He knew I saw Him too. As this vision was ending, I heard a song in the recesses of my mind: "Here Comes the Sun" (1969) by the Beatles.

> *I [the Lord] will instruct you and teach you in the way you should go; I will counsel you with My eye upon you.*
>
> **—Psalm 32:8 AMPC**

In 1987, as part of my art degree, I had to come up with a marketing strategy to sell a product. I designed a cereal box and had drawn a coupon on a flyer. I had drawn a little girl and boy sitting in a cave, looking out with binoculars. The name of the cereal was "Unicorns," so they were scoping out the environment for this creature. It seems I came full circle on that vision. Only God! Here I am thirty years later, looking into the unseen realm for Heaven's perspective once again.

Around this time, many of Dr. Kevin Zadai's conferences were in Conroe, Texas, and I was able to attend them. I saw a man get hit by the power of God and fly right out of his wheelchair. It was remarkable because he went so far up and came down in a somersault, landing in the audience. Yet, the more astounding part was when I found out who the man was. He was a pastor from San Antonio who had licensed and ordained me in 2004 at his church.

Interestingly enough, the church's name was Alpha and Omega. Could my open vision of the alpha sign be a reminder of that very commission? This pastor and his wife spent some time catching up with me. They now reside in Magnolia, Texas. He had also miraculously been healed of cancer several years earlier. Then he said the most beautiful thing: "You've always been under our covering." What a sweet blessing. This couple was in their nineties and still going strong for Jesus. Hallelujah!

My husband had been very supportive up to this point. Not realizing that he was quite the discerner himself, I believed that I was the only spiritual one in our family. He and I had locked arms with a church in Illinois during the fall of 2019. We had already visited four times to see Dr. Zadai's live conferences there. Doug would set up all the chairs for the venue, and I would walk through the aisles, blessing the area, praying over every seat, and anointing the entire building with oil. The pastor at this church relied heavily on us when we were around. We had absolutely no problem with this, and we were grateful to serve. I made a few friends there whom I still talk to even now.

In the spring of 2022, Holy Spirit gave us both dreams and visions to let us know something was off. After watching this ministry's online conferences a few times, I dreamed that I was out in the middle of the ocean, and waves were crashing up on the shore. There was a huge red beach ball being tossed around. Red signifies the blood, power, and prophetic anointing.

Out of nowhere, a woman approached me, holding an unusually large diamond, as if it were the crown jewel of a kingdom. She expected me to take it as she handed it to me. One quick glance, and I knew in my spirit that it was a fake. As I cradled this "diamond" in my palm for a moment, the Spirit spoke louder; nothing about it felt authentic, so I returned it to her immediately. She turned around and disappeared into the water. Then the dream ended.

A few negative interactions with a leader at this church shortly after the dream were enough for my husband and me to separate from the church. At the time, leadership had been discussing licensing and ordaining us both. I had just begun my second two-year term in Bible college under their ministry and was concerned that I might not graduate. Yet, God's boundless grace made the path clear for me. I could continue my studies online, and by His faithful provision, I graduated with a diploma in Christian Ministry by the end of the program in November 2022.

A few weeks after I had that dream, during an online prayer meeting, the leader called out my name. "And God would say, 'You are My diamond. You go for the real. You don't reach for the fake.'" Well, that was confirmation enough for me. We believed the Spirit had led us to move on. Several months later, it was confirmed by others who had left the congregation.

On the topic of diamonds, I had another intense and prophetic dream. In this dream, two large dragonflies flew out of my kitchen onto the back patio. I immediately noticed several young adults full of joy and laughter riding in a red convertible Volkswagen Beetle.

I then saw that our swimming pool was completely empty. The water had formed a tornado-like whirlwind and was spinning like a top in our yard. But it wasn't just water; it looked as if it were crystals or diamonds. Now, I had seen water in my dreams before, but nothing like this. I felt strongly that my husband and I were digging wells of revival here in our home.

Shortly after this dream, the Lord would bring me several young women who wanted discipleship. I had taken on twelve young women during the time Covid-19 had forced many of the AA meeting places to close their doors.

But, back to the diamond tornado. Diamonds are brilliant; they attract; they are hard. According to Arizona State University, when the pressure is about 50,000 times the pressure at the surface of the Earth and the temperature is about 1600 degrees Celsius, the carbon atoms bond with four other atoms and result in diamonds.[7] These precious rare stones are found and collected near the surface of the Earth in special volcanic ground called kimberlite. (No coincidence there.)

7. Arizona State University.

As the weeks went by, I began watching more and more of Dr. Kevin Zadai's videos. Students were given an invitation by the dean, Pastor Mike Cowen, to start a Warrior Fellowship. A fellowship's meeting would include a short teaching from Dr. Zadai and then time to discuss the teaching. We would then be expected to pray for each other and to pray for the individual needs of the attendees. Was I up for the challenge?

Living out in the Hill Country, I was concerned there would be very little attendance. Still, we followed our hearts and began Warrior Fellowship of Mico, Texas. I finally found what I was looking for: people who believed like I did and wanted more of what God had to offer. I hadn't really grasped the concept of synchronization just yet. I just knew in my heart that we were being led to do more and give more of ourselves to the ministry.

An uptick in my dream encounters and visions began as the fellowship began to grow. Drs. Kevin or Kathi Zadai would mention a topic at one of the sessions during their Spirit schools, and I would have already seen it played out in the weeks or days prior.

Once I dreamed that Dr. Kevin was walking through a very long narrow corridor resembling a human artery. His hands were on the ceiling, as if he was holding on tightly. I even noticed the limp he has on one side. He later announced on a live broadcast that he had walked into the Father's heart. I got a quickening in my spirit as soon as he shared this. Why would the Lord allow me to see this preemptively? Maybe it was an invitation to follow him there. Indeed, I would follow—blaze a trail, is more like it.

Toward the end of my nine-year tenure in the school district, I dreamed I was wading through the hallways of my high school. I looked down to see the water was brown and thick, like a swamp. I saw waste in the water. I had to lift my legs up high over all the sewage and propel myself forward. It was a struggle, and it felt as though it was taking forever. I got to the base of a stairway and began climbing to the second floor. At the top of the stairwell, there was another hallway.

The scene changed, and now the second level was clean and bright. I spotted my desk in a room. I walked over to the desk, took off my shoes, and placed them into the bottom drawer. I was given a brand-new pair of white patent leather shoes to put on. After placing them on my feet, I walked out an exit door. The sun was shining, and there was a fire truck waiting outside for me. There were some of the fire academy students gathered around. I looked intently at the fire truck. The fire hose came loose all on its own and was aimed right at me. Instead of shooting me with water, an enormous blast of pink confetti came streaming out of the nozzle. Then the dream ended.

Well, wouldn't you know? It was just as the Lord had shown me. A demonic yet unseen force began to permeate the halls and the souls of an unexpected and unknowing faculty. I could now see that I was dealing with an entire group of people who didn't even mind being deceived. In fact, some of them welcomed it. This was preposterous to me. How can anyone welcome a socialist agenda? One where free will is nonexistent?

The ending of this dream really perplexed me; I struggled for months afterward. I was trying to figure out what the confetti was all about, and I could only conclude that God had a surprise waiting for me in the future. Fast forward three years to May 2024. I realized that when you completed all your course requirements, on the ministry school website, confetti shot out around your certificate of completion. It was just one more confirmation that I was tracking with God's plans for my life. I was becoming that fire hose.

Another time I dreamed someone was skeet shooting. I saw these disks flying up into the air one after another. Someone was shooting them right out of the sky. That same evening while watching Dr. Kevin, he shared that he had been at the shooting range and described the exact scene I had dreamed about. I felt as though the Holy Spirit was saying, "Here I am. Interested yet?" Like playing a game of holy hide and seek, I had to do the seeking in order to find what was hiding. "Jehovah Sneaky" has a tendency to lay down a trail of breadcrumbs for me to follow. When I am diligent in searching out the Scriptures, He is mighty to pour out His abundance of wisdom and understanding.

The following week I had another dream. I was riding my bicycle through a neighborhood. I parked my bike and began walking through an area that looked exactly like our school's courtyard. I could tell there was a neighborhood being erected. It was a construction zone. I walked down a path that led to a huge carved wooden door. On the top of the door was a plaque that read "Dr. Wu." I opened the door as if I had an appointment. The receptionist gave me a hard time, and we got into an argument. I left abruptly and thought, *Wow! These people are no help at all.* I suspected that they were doing something bad there. Then the dream ended.

I found out later that some philanthropists had come in and convinced our school district to manage Covid-19. We were called to a special meeting one Saturday afternoon via Zoom. There was a keynote speaker there to instruct all the nurses how to manage and trace Covid-19. She was the health expert from the Metropolitan Health District. Wouldn't you know, her name was Dr. Wu! Some of the nurses were expressing their displeasure with what our new duties entailed. They even managed to get our superintendent to give us a $500 increase. None of them had enough conviction to say, "No! Not on my watch!" The pay increase sealed the deal. That dream was a warning about what was being built up around us, right down to the person's name. The Holy Spirit had been showing me what was going on behind the scenes once again.

About six months later, Warrior Notes came to San Antonio to do a one-night event. I believe having Dr. Kevin and his team there really upset some high-level devils. When you are walking in your God-given authority and you know it, you can disrupt a multitude of high-ranking demons. I had been the school nurse at a San Antonio high school for the past nine years. I absolutely loved my job. The anointing on me became a threat to a whole new administrative team that had come in. Covid-19 was making everyone paranoid. Some staff members were getting three and four vaccines. Everyone was forced to wear masks. The workload became unbearable. We had been forced to trace the virus outside the four walls of the school. I was at my wit's end. Little did I know, my assistant had turned her back on me and was plotting to have me let go.

A few days later at work, a freshman came into the clinic after having cut her wrists up and down with a sharp blade. I washed her arms with soap and water and patted them dry. Leaning into her softly I asked her if I could pray for her.

"No! I'm an atheist. In fact, my family and I worship satan!" Not wanting to push the issue, I bandaged her up and sent her on her way. My comment must have upset her so much that she went and reported me to the principal. Not only was I written up, but the family notified the superintendent and asked to have me let go.

My boss at health services had my back, and I was not fired. However, my new assistant had gone behind my back and written up a contradictory statement, falsely accusing me of forcing prayer on students and on her. My manager tried her best to get us to continue working together in the clinic.

What hurt the most was that my assistant testified against me. I had spent all year training her. I knew this was no longer a safe environment to be in. How can you work alongside someone you know has lied about your character? I was given the option to transfer to another high school on the east side of town, but after much prayer and counsel, I chose to resign from the district. God had prepared me in advance by giving me the dream. The lesson learned here was that once someone has shot an arrow at you, that cannot be undone. I knew my Lord would heal the wound, but I could no longer stay in that role. They weren't rejecting me. They were rejecting the Holy Spirit who was residing within me.

Can God use an act of betrayal to build your character and move you closer to destiny? I was about to find out.

I never thought in a million years that my faith would lead me to this. What was I going to do now? The stress in my home was overwhelming. Could we make it on one salary? The skills needed to do school nursing are very different from those of a hospital nurse. I applied for jobs in other school districts and found nothing. Although school nurses are grossly underpaid, we enjoy weekends home with our families and summers to recoup. I started to think God no longer had me covered.

There is something about financial insecurity that is so evil, if you don't address it head on, it is liable to take you down fast. Thank the Lord for godly counsel and friends who poured into us. But truly, Dr. Zadai's teaching on supernatural finance really spoke to us the loudest.

My husband and I, as a couple, listened very closely to the teachings on "Supernatural Finances." Besides leading the fellowships every week, we turned our home into an outreach center. We began collecting clothing, food, blankets, and toiletries for anyone who needed them. Then, suddenly, things shifted again.

Chapter 10

DRAFTED INTO WAR

A simple bag of groceries turned into a divine appointment seven miles from home. My husband decided that he was going to bless one of our neighbors with a bag of groceries. He packed up a bunch of food into his car and included a copy of Dr. Kevin Zadai's book *Heavenly Visitation* (2015). We delivered this package to Diane, who lived about seven miles away. We met her through the church and lost touch with her during Covid-19. She was so overwhelmed when my husband delivered the food and book. He also took the time to pray with her and her two older adult children who were there visiting. It was beautiful to witness.

What really amazed me, though, was when, exactly fourteen days later, a client walked into my husband's place of employment. He told my husband how much he valued his assistance over the years before offering my husband a career managing his 250-acre ranch. This position would include a $35,000 increase in his salary. This small act of human kindness and compassion, with no ulterior motive, started a domino effect in our financial life that we never saw coming. The divine timing of this change allowed me to be a stay-at-home mom to our now twelve-year-old daughter.

> *"Bring the whole tithe into the storehouse, that there may be food in my house. Test me in this," says the Lord Almighty, "and see if I will not throw open the floodgates of heaven and pour out so much blessing that there will not be room enough to store it."*
>
> **—Malachi 3:10 NIV**

Since then, my husband and I have watched the courses titled "Warrior Marketplace," which are offered by Warrior Notes School of Ministry. My husband began hearing from the Lord on a new business idea almost immediately. The Lord showed him a prototype for a piece of equipment and even gave him the entire layout of the building that would house the warehouse, factory, supplies, and business center. He laid out every architectural detail in a vivid panoramic vision. Doug followed Holy Spirit's lead and recently completed the prototype.

> *Then the Lord replied: "Write down the revelation and make it plain on tablets so that a herald may run with it. For the revelation awaits an appointed time;*

it speaks of the end and will not prove false. Though it linger, wait for it; it will certainly come and will not delay."

—Habakkuk 2:2–3 NIV

This is one of my favorite Scriptures from the minor prophets. According to Hitchcock's Bible names dictionary, the name *Habakkuk* actually means "he that embraces."[8] I wrote down the revelations, and boy, did I embrace them! I ran with them! I had no idea that in just a few short years, everything I was seeing would somehow come to pass. Some dreams did become reality rather quickly. Some of the dreams are now unfolding in ways I never thought imaginable. Some I am still patiently waiting for.

Habakkuk gave encouragement to Judah in her time of crisis. The Lord has captured me with encouragement in these current times of crisis by giving me snapshots of the future and directing me to pray for specific outcomes. He has given us all the keys, and as good stewards, we must keep His vision close to our hearts. It is well known in Christian circles that *Judah* means "praise." I have learned to praise Him in good times and in bad times. He has never reneged on His promises.

Soon after leaving the school district in September 2021, I was able to concentrate on all the courses that Warrior Notes was releasing. It was such an honor and a privilege to see that

8. Roswell D. Hitchcock, *An Interpreting Dictionary of Scripture Proper Names,* s.v., "Habakkuk" (New York, 1869).

confetti fly all around my computer screen every time I finished a course.

As the old saying goes, "All is fair in love and war." Well, I had no idea that this loving God of mine had drafted me into war.

> *For the weapons of our warfare are not carnal, but mighty through God to the pulling down of strong holds.*
>
> **—2 Corinthians 10:4 KJV**

What I didn't realize then was that I was still at war with myself and others. I was watching a Warrior Notes conference one evening and decided I would chime in on the live YouTube chat. You can get really bold on the other end of those things, knowing you can say whatever comes to mind and nobody is there to censor or correct you. But the Holy Spirit knows.

> *For the Spirit searches all things, yes, the deep things of God.*
>
> **—1 Corinthians 2:10b**

As I mentioned earlier, the sanctification process is long and can take a lifetime. We are never perfect, but we serve a perfect

God. I suppose He felt that this was a good time for me to learn some things about myself. I had just put in the chat, "Give me more humility, Lord!" If I recall correctly, someone replied in the chat, "Oh my! Don't pray for that!"

I chuckled to myself and thought, *What could be so bad about that?* Well, little did I know that my entire family was planning an intervention that evening. They were just waiting for the right time to let me know what they thought. After the conference ended, I stepped into the living room to find my entire family sitting there, waiting for me. They had elected my oldest daughter to be the spokesperson. Apparently, everyone was fed up with me not listening to them. They said I didn't pay attention to them and would even talk over them. This was a hard pill to swallow. *What kind of minister doesn't listen well or allow others to speak?* I repented and asked for help with what I couldn't do alone. I was a work in progress.

Years later, Dr. Kevin shared that we should never ask God to humble us. If we do, we are headed for a smackdown. God will humble us before the day's end because He was on a schedule, and we are way behind the curve. The apostle Paul's teachings urge us to judge ourselves so God won't have to. Fall on the rock, lest the rock fall on you (see Matthew 21:44). Lesson learned!

Moving into 2022, I was connected to another "Warrior woman" through a mutual friend in the fellowship. We had one conversation. Toward the end of our talk, she asked if she could sing me a song. It was the most beautiful song I had ever heard. It was hard to believe it was an original song, but it was. When she finished singing, she said, "And the Lord would have you know, He is teaching you when to speak and when to be silent." I wept. I know that He is the God who sees, my Jehovah El Roi.

> *Jesus did many other things as well. If every one of them were written down, I suppose that even the whole world would not have room for the books that would be written.*
>
> **—John 21:25 NIV**

By then, dreams were coming almost nightly. I was seeing and hearing like never before. I began writing them all down, but I honestly could not even keep up. Something supernatural would happen several times a day. There seemed to be one common thread throughout my dreams: Warrior Notes.

One particular dream really stood out. I was in a stadium with thousands of people. I am in the audience looking up to the stage. The next thing I know, two women are leading me up to the front by my arms. I seem to be excited yet leery. I looked at the woman on my left and said, "How am I supposed to do this?" She looked at me and said, "Here, put this on." She handed me what seemed to be warrior garb. It was a full suit of armor—helmet, shield, and all. The armor was supernaturally placed on my body, and both women continued leading me up to the front of the stage.

> *Put on God's whole armor [the armor of a heavy-armed soldier which God supplies], that you may be able successfully to stand up against [all] the strategies and the deceits of the devil.*
>
> **—Ephesians 6:11 AMPC**

Soon I was diving into all the courses that the Warrior Notes School of Ministry had to offer. "The Weapons of Our Warfare" course would bring new hope and meaning to that dream of mine. This was the beginning of a new stage in my spiritual journey. By enrolling in the courses and dedicating my time to learning, I began to sense and feel that these teachings had become a reality in my life. God was no longer an iconic concept; He was my ever-present help in times of trouble (see Psalm 46:1). The more I studied and devoted my life to seeking the Lord, the more encounters and experiences I had.

One evening I was thinking, as I often do, *I've already been to school. I have three degrees already. What is the point of all this?* That very evening as I slept, I had a dream. In it, I saw a runner on a racetrack. I was following him as he passed all the other contestants. I clearly saw him pass the baton to me. He crossed the finish line. Then the dream ended.

In the summer of 2022, I graduated with my Warrior Notes School of Ministry associate's degree in Conroe, Texas. It was a huge surprise to find that Dr. Zadai had purchased gold batons and distributed them to all the grads that day.

Talk about dreams coming true! I will never regret my decision to pick up that baton and run—run, run, run—until I cross that finish line. I want to go up like Elijah. I want to be an Enoch, a Paul, a Deborah in my generation. If a flight attendant went out of his way to leave Heaven and come back to earth so we could have the answers to the test, I think I'm going to take him up on it—all of it. Being yoked to Dr. Zadai's ministry has completely changed the trajectory of my life.

Around this time, I had been participating in an online group based out of Denton, Texas, that was connected to the ministry. We met every Friday evening via Zoom, and through those gatherings, I formed several close friendships within the Warrior Notes community. I was also regularly hosting a small group in my home every Sunday afternoon. After about a year and a half, my husband and I decided to open it up to a wider audience by offering it on Zoom as well.

We were surprised to see people from other countries, such as India and Africa, as well as people from other states join us. Even today, we have a gentleman from Canada whom we look forward to seeing every week. We have become like family. We began seeing miracle after miracle. On some nights the holy laughter would kick in. Someone would start off, and we would just be howling and literally rolling around on the floor. Holy laughter is good medicine!

One Friday night while attending the Denton Warrior Fellowship, the leader decided to change the format. Rather than watching the video, she decided we were going to pray first.

We all began to give our prayer requests. I raised my hand, and I asked for prayer for my stepchildren. I had been feeling insecure about the relationship, and I could sense my children were under attack. I got honest with my feelings about inadequacy and shared a little bit about the challenges that I was going through.

That weekend, all our children were over and had gathered in the living room, where my husband was keeping an eye on them. I had closed off my room to avoid interruptions. Not two minutes later, my stepson Connor comes barreling in the room and asks me if I can pray for him because he is being bullied at school. I was in complete awe at how quickly my prayers began to be answered. I had him sit in my chair so that the people in the fellowship could see him on camera and begin praying for him. He began confessing all of his problems, and the prayers just came rolling out of the computer screen. He began weeping, and I knew God was working.

When the group finished praying, Connor went back to the living room to join his two sisters. They were all just sitting around watching television. Not five minutes later, my husband bursts in the door and says, "Kim, you have to see this!"

My stepdaughter Madison was giving godly counseling to Connor about his behavior, and he was just sitting there listening to her, which he never does. My husband also mentioned that my oldest daughter, Brooke, was in the restroom with the door slightly open, listening in. He could tell that she was being deeply moved by what Madison was sharing with Connor. Not only were they loving and supporting one another, they were talking about God. This was miraculous.

Could the residue of what was happening in the online fellowship in one room seep over into the next room and be strong enough to convict my entire household? You had better believe it! This is what happens when you allow the glory of God to come into your home and His presence take up residence. Glory be to God!

God never disappoints. He is always ready and willing to show Himself strong. It has become my goal to really give the devil a headache. I started a YouTube channel to share the supernatural events we experienced at our fellowship. I had gotten to be very close friends with another "Warrior woman" from Denton, Texas. She encouraged me to branch out and try online ministry. It was just me, sharing my experience, strength, and hope with the body of Christ.

One evening our group had gone over the usual two-hour fellowship. People had traveled to our home from San Antonio, which was a good hour drive away. We were having an amazing time, and I certainly did not want to prohibit the Holy Spirit from working. One of my personal friends brought his autistic son. I could sense that the Spirit was willing, so we prayed for his complete healing. Freedom had come, and everyone was on fire. It was much like the upper room experience described in the book of Acts.

My friends and I continued to pray for several hours that day. Eventually, we were caught off guard by the arrival of four fire trucks as they parked right in front of my home. Our neighbors had called the fire department because they saw flames coming from the roof of our house. We spent the remainder of that day watching outside as the firefighters frantically looked all over ours and the surrounding properties for a fire. They could find nothing. Intuitively, I knew exactly what had occurred.

> *For our God is a consuming fire.*
>
> **—Hebrews 12:29**

Chapter 11

GOD LOVES BIRDS

Bills didn't care about layoffs, and neither did the future. After losing my job as a school nurse, it felt like the ground fell out beneath my feet. Nursing was all I had known. My husband and I lay awake night after night, tossing around half-baked ideas, desperate for a way forward. Then, like a whisper in the chaos, I remembered something Dr. Kevin had said more than once: "Go back to your first love." That's when it hit me: birds. As a child, I was obsessed with them. I was fascinated by their colors, their voices, their freedom. With the last of our savings, I convinced my husband to take a leap with me: we'd buy, breed, and sell exotic birds. We did our research and discovered there wasn't much competition in our area. This could work! It sounded wild. It sounded risky. But how hard could it be?

We had heard of a place in Corpus Christi called Feathered Friends & Co. We checked in with the owner periodically to make sure baby parrots were in stock. Doug and I made the decision together to take that long drive south. We found a cheap hotel room and rented it, planning to stay just until we could wake up the next day and be there when the pet shop opened. As we were unpacking our bags, I glanced out the window and saw Jesus standing out on a boat. We chuckled because we had settled in right next to the First United Methodist Church and its figure of Jesus. "It is I" was inscribed on the bottom portion of this sculpture.

> *But immediately he spoke to them and said, "Take heart, it is I; have no fear."*
>
> **—Mark 6:50b RSV**

There are no coincidences in my life—only God incidents. This was a "God wink" for me. We drove to the store and proceeded to buy a beautiful conure whom we named Penny Lynn.

> *And the Lord added....*
>
> **—Acts 2:47b**

We wound up making several trips to this location because of their vast selection. We believed if we had two of every kind, they would eventually multiply. It wasn't long before my husband closed the door on the ark. Not only were these birds not multiplying, but they were also jealous of one another. All this squawking and no mating! Could it have been self-will?

Not realizing it, these birds were not warming up to us because they were not hand tamed. After watching a few videos and realizing that we had spent all our money on these birds that would never warm up to us, I was crushed. I hadn't done enough research on the matter. I had to get several cages and place the birds separately for them to get along. Bird cages now crowded the already small sunroom we had chosen to keep them in.

One day while scrolling through Facebook, my husband came across a woman from Conroe, Texas, who was selling baby cockatiels. By now, we were used to driving to Conroe for conferences. I think my husband felt bad and knew that I wanted a domesticated bird I could love, so he agreed to drive me there one afternoon. We came home with the most adorable, all white, male lutino cockatiel. We hand-fed him until he was able to eat on his own. We watched as he flew for the first time. A special bond formed between him and me. His name is Mr. Bingley. He always chimes in when the Holy Spirit is present. He is teachable and loves to sing and dance.

I know the song says, "Make me a house of prayer," not "make me a house of birds," but there is just something so pure and beautiful about them.[9]

About four months after weaning this little guy, my daughter was walking outside and not paying attention. When she

9. Eddie James, artist, "House of Prayer," *Shift (Awakening)* album, Fresh Wine Records, 2014.

opened the door, Mr. Bingley flew out. I was devastated. It was a very windy day, and the wind just seemed to sweep him away.

My soul was crushed, but my heart was saying, "Jesus, I trust in You." I did the only thing that I knew to do, and that was to go and help someone else. It always eases my pain to help another person. So, my husband and I packed up and headed for San Antonio. We picked up my mother and took her out for the evening. I focused my attention on being a good daughter. I had said some not-so-choice words to my daughter when it happened, but I immediately apologized and then I forgave her with all my heart. I had learned to forgive at once, in order to move forward in life.

Later that evening my husband put an ad on a local social media platform called Next Door. It was very short. He left Mr. Bingley's description and a phone number and included the fact that he was very tame and would land on your head.

The next morning, I thought I would make myself useful and chip away the old paint on our deck handrails. It was very hot that July morning, and the Texas sun was beaming. As I began to open a new gallon of paint, my husband came running out into the backyard.

"Get your shoes on and grab your keys!" he shouted. I didn't ask questions. I just did what he said.

We got into the car and drove three miles. My husband pulled up to a driveway and next to it stood a massive white rock. No address, just a rock. "This is it!" he exclaimed.

Driving up this very long driveway, I looked up to see a middle-aged couple standing outside their cabin. The woman had Mr. Bingley on top of her head. "We read your ad this morning, and as we walked outside, this little fellow landed on my wife's head," the husband stated. Words cannot explain the overwhelming joy and gratitude that flowed out that day.

In the meantime, I had been hiding the fact that I organized a fishing getaway for my husband and me to celebrate our anniversary, which was July 7th, the very next day. I had found a little cabin on a lake where my husband could relax and I could do what I like to do, which is to commune with God. It was so perfect. The water came right up to the deck of the cabin. Doug could fish from the front porch. This was a dream come true for him.

On our getaway, we enjoyed a nice dinner at a local Italian restaurant and returned to our rental. While Doug was fishing from the deck, I had been scrolling through Facebook and came upon an interview between Kelsey O'Malley and Kim Robinson. I had seen Kelsey speak at one of Dr. Kevin Zadai's conferences in Phoenix. I had never heard of Kim Robinson. What stood out was her name: Kim, like mine, and robin in her last name, like the bird.

Kim was talking about an encounter she had with Jesus while out on a fishing trip, describing a setting that was very close to what I was experiencing at that moment. Then she shared that the Father was holding a little bird on the tip of His finger. He was petting the bird and kissed its little head. Then God looked at her and said, "I love birds!" But when He said this, she felt all of creation move. It was so powerful, it blew her hair back and reverberated through her entire being.

While I was listening to her testimony, this same powerful shock wave came right through the phone and blasted me. Once again, I felt that weighted blanket of love enveloping me. I was plastered to the bed. All I could think of was, *He loves birds, and He heard my cry. He returned my baby Bingley to me within 24 hours.* I wept and wept for hours. I could not have held back my tears if I had tried. I knew beyond a shadow of a doubt that was for me. The divine timing on that broadcast and getting my sweet bird back the day before had been orchestrated by my Father. God is always right on time. What a way to celebrate our anniversary.

Not even one year later, my youngest daughter was so excited by the arrival of her siblings, she swung open the front door, not realizing that Mr. Bingley was out. Once again, he flew right out the door. Oh my goodness, not again. God was merciful one time, but would He do it again? You better believe He would. I had been immediately struck with fear; however, I said out loud, "Jesus, I trust in You." I asked my husband to put another ad in Next Door, which he did. The very next day, I was looking at the cedar shavings on the bottom of the cage. To my surprise, Holly, our female cockatiel, had laid an egg. Would it be viable? Did God give us this precious baby to carry on Mr. Bingley's legacy? Although I was excited to see that egg, I missed my little guy.

On the third day, I woke up with a heavy heart. I couldn't seem to pull it together. I had to force myself to get out of bed and get moving. My faith was beginning to waver. Just then, my husband called. "Take down this address, hurry up, and get there—they found Mr. Bingley!" I immediately got dressed and jumped in the car.

It was four long miles to where he ended up. I pulled up to what was obviously a large ranch. With so many animals, he could have easily become a snack! The owner came out with a huge box in his hands. He explained to me that he had gone out to feed the dogs and found Mr. Bingley in the dog kennel. The dogs had been inside their home overnight because of all the rain. Had it not rained, this story might have ended differently. I've heard it said that rain is a blessing. It sure was for us. Once again, I got my little birdie back. Only God! He is so faithful.

Warrior Notes held a conference in Pensacola, Florida, in late 2024. I had no intentions of going, and I certainly had no financial resources at the time. A warrior sister called me less than a month earlier and suggested we go together. Something (God) in my spirit told me, "You are going." The next night, I had an encounter with the Spirit of God. I first saw a huge bag of birdseed. The next scene was eight or nine birds perched on a long branch. I said, "Lord, why are all these birds perched here in my kitchen?" He said, "Because you are feeding them." That same day, my husband came home from work carrying an enormous bag of wild birdseed into the house.

Toward the end of that week, my mom gave me the money for the airfare, a gift that I never saw coming. Two weeks prior to leaving, I got a call from that same Warrior sister telling me she couldn't go but that she would connect me to a friend who lived in Orlando, who had also planned on going to the conference. This would require us to drive from Orlando to Pensacola, which is a two-hour drive, depending on traffic. It felt awkward because I didn't know this friend of hers, but I had already purchased the plane tickets and they were non-refundable, so I agreed to go.

The woman, Becky, picked me up from the airport, and I could instantly feel her love and acceptance. Who does this? Who agrees to pick up a stranger and live with that person for three days in an Airbnb? That was meant to be. When we got to her house, I walked into the kitchen, and no sooner did I look up than I saw that same picture of the birds perched on that branch in her dining room. There was also a beautiful stream running through her backyard. It felt like I had walked into paradise. The view was breathtaking. I instantly knew this was a divine appointment.

She knew nothing about me, yet she had prepared all our food in advance. Several portions of beef and other proteins were portioned out. The veggies were already washed, cut up, and packed neatly into portable storage containers. She even had coffee and cream, just the way I like it, packed and ready to go in the back of her hatchback. A tailgate party! I view my body as God's temple and don't just eat whatever is placed in front of me. Becky didn't know this, but God knew.

But my God shall supply all your need according to his riches in glory by Christ Jesus.

—Philippians 4:19 KJV

If you don't believe that God can supply all your need, you may never go forward or advance the kingdom. That's another one of those foundational building blocks I gladly accepted early on in my transformation.

The icing on the cake would have to be the third day of the conference. It was Sunday afternoon, and we were driving back to Orlando so that I could catch an evening flight. As we were driving over the intercoastal highway, a pelican came right up to my window as I was seated on the passenger front seat. The pelican flew right next to my head for about a solid minute. It was so beautiful to see this creature traveling side by side with me. His beak was enormous.

My mom loves pelicans. She told me a story one year about why she loved these birds so much. Of course, she had been living in Miami when she became pregnant with me, and I'm sure she saw many of them herself. Pelicans will take their own flesh and feed it to their babies to prevent them from starving. This is a prophetic picture of what Jesus Christ did for us at the cross. I also ponder the idea that the pelican's beak can hold so many fish. This is what I like to refer to as a "calling experience." God is calling, and He draws you into an experience to show you exactly where you are heading.

Chapter 12

LINKED AND SYNCED

There comes a moment in every believer's journey when the Spirit whispers, "It's time to go deeper."

By 2024, I found myself standing at the threshold of a new dimension of personal growth—not by my own striving, but by divine summons. I could feel the Lord calling me higher, asking for more.

> *...To whom much is given, from him much will be required... .*
>
> **—Luke 12:48**

This wasn't just about maturity; it was about surrendering. The season had come for sacrifice, and I began to walk the road of deeper obedience. When the Lord said, "Minister," I didn't hesitate. I moved.

In those moments of yieldedness, I started to see how the Holy Spirit weaves visions and discernment together, not for spectacle, but for deliverance. Through simple obedience, I was learning how God partners with His people to set the captives free.

It's easy to tithe when you have an income and money in the bank. It is another thing to sacrifice your time and resources when you yourself don't have much to give. Obedience and personal sacrifice are a vital part of living a life that is pleasing to God. I am no longer just a fan; I have become sold out for God.

In June 2025, I had a four-part series dream. The scene began in a pristine kitchen adorned in blue and white. As I looked around, I found myself truly admiring the beauty of the space. The intricate blue-and-white tile work stood out; blue, to me, has always symbolized revelation, Heaven, and faith in the spiritual realm. That the dream took place in a kitchen could reflect my spiritual appetite—both to be fed and to feed others through teaching and preaching.

I found myself facing north when I noticed two faint, circular stains by the sink—remnants of coffee cups. As I began to wipe them away, the stains lifted easily, almost effortlessly, filling me with quiet joy. Then I turned to the window facing east, took hold of both curtain panels, and drew them back, allowing the light to pour in. It was a moment that felt like a gentle unveiling, both in the natural and the spiritual.

The dream transitioned, and I began turning around to face the opposite wall. Suddenly, someone who I could not see was pouring salt from a saltshaker all over my face and hair. A very concentrated amount of salt was pouring over my mouth. The sun shone down over my entire being.

Then the dream changed again. I turned my attention in another direction, facing south, in the same kitchen, and as I did, a large oak tree came busting out of the wall. It was as if this tree had arms and punched its way through the sheetrock.

> *In those days and at that time I will make a righteous Branch sprout from David's line.*
>
> **—Jeremiah 33:15a NIV**

I was examining this oak tree when I noticed one single monarch butterfly had perched on one of the branches. Monarch butterflies are a powerful symbol of transformation and divine change, often reflecting the work of the Spirit in renewing, refining, and leading us into a new season. Then I woke up. At first, the dream didn't seem like anything particularly significant. But then, something happened the very next day that brought it into focus.

I began my morning by catching up on a Warrior Notes conference as school required. Dr. Kevin was in Dallas and had a panel of two male guests speaking with him. I walked over to my kitchen to find two brown marks on my counter just like the ones I had dreamed about, and I was relieved to find they wiped off easily. As I was experiencing this weird déjà vu, I looked up and saw Dr. Kevin's guest saying, "I pulled back the curtains in the kitchen, and all this light flooded in." He had described my dream to a T!

Not one or two days later, I'm watching an older broadcast of Dr. Zadai's. I believe he was in Waupun at the time. He started talking about the Holy Spirit coming in and covering us with a healthy dose of salt on our lips. Each segment of that dream, one right after the other, was being played out for me. If that is not being in sync with the Spirit of a living God, then I don't know what is.

Several weeks later while attending another Warrior Notes Spirit School in Conroe, Texas, I was listening to "Finding Your Sweet Spot." I opened Facebook because I was going to share the link with a friend. To my surprise, there is a post of Snoopy in the same kitchen from my dream. The blue and white checkered tile, the sun shining through the window, and even the two coffee cups were there. The Holy Spirit does these things to confirm His voice and His leadings. How can you doubt or have disbelief when you are encountering the living God in this manner? My sweet spot today has become a place I never want to leave: it is being wrapped up in Jesus.

Soon afterward, during a trip to Melville, New York, I exited the plane at LaGuardia airport and saw a large print of that same oak tree with the butterfly perched on it. Something sparks inside of me when I see the supernatural manifesting in front of me. I can always see and sense the angels around me and others. This trip to another Warrior Notes Spirit School was no exception. I had seen most of the journey played out in dreams weeks before we left. God had shown me the topic of the conference. While in the hotel room, the Holy Spirit gave me another dream, which included another book title and cover design.

I saw a few stores we would be visiting, right down to the cashiers. He showed me there would be trouble on a bridge. I was able to pray against satan's plans and schemes beforehand. When that trouble came, as I knew it would, God made a safe way off the bridge so my daughter and I would make our return flight just in the nick of time.

During a visit to my mother in San Antonio, I experienced a profound moment. I had parked in her driveway and was praying with a friend in my car, outside her home, planning to take her to a doctor's appointment. After praying for over thirty minutes, I opened my mother's front door only to find her standing there with a blank look on her face. She was diaphoretic and had a grayish pallor. She staggered to the kitchen and collapsed. Her pupils were fixed and dilated, and I knew she was close to death. I noticed the time on her microwave oven was 11:11 am. This time always reminds me of Hebrews 11:1 (KJV): "Now faith is the substance of things hoped for, the evidence of things not seen."

I felt a sense of calm, but then a righteous anger came over me. I prayed fervently, commanding her soul to return to her body. After what felt like an eternity—twenty agonizing minutes—she finally stirred. With a groan, she rolled onto her side and retched violently, spewing a surge of green bile onto the floor. My heart pounded as I rushed to her side, lifting her trembling body and helping her onto the couch. She collapsed into the cushions, pale and weak, but breathing. I sat beside her, overwhelmed with relief, and whispered a silent prayer of thanks—grateful beyond words for God's mercy in that moment. She had no idea how close she came to leaving this earth. She looked at me, smiling, with a completely positive attitude, and asked if I would go get her a hamburger.

I still have my mother, and I am grateful for every moment we spend together. If all our days have been numbered and all our steps ordered, then there's no way I'm going to let the enemy and his minions have his way in my life or in the lives of those He has entrusted to me.

Soon after that, while watching one of Dr. Kevin's conferences, he was sharing about a similar experience. He had prayed for someone to come back to life. His exact words were, "Bring them back to life and then give them a hamburger!" I'm telling you, I can't make this stuff up!

Learning to follow Holy Spirit and release my plans and dreams to Him has been an adventure. Sometimes it is easy to focus on my wants and pursue what I believe is important at the time. There eventually comes the moment when I see God's sovereign hand behind it all. Once again, I am humbled. I am grateful to be a soldier in God's end-time army.

My husband is bombarded with these occurrences daily also. I don't know what we ever did to deserve this kind of supernatural life. I guess it's not about deserving it or earning it. I am beginning to realize that this is God's normal. This is what it looks like to be walking hand and hand with the Maker of the universe. When we give God our "yes," He honors that. I am sure that the trajectory of my life and my family's life has changed forever.

The question is, will you agree with God? I believe He has something better for all of us. I had to learn to get myself ready for it. Learning to pass the test of waiting for God's guidance is no simple feat. But you also can't start praying when you are being thrown into the trenches. We all must learn how to walk in two realms if we are to live victoriously in this life.

Chapter 13

PROMISES FOR OBEDIENCE

Have you ever eavesdropped on a conversation at the table next to you? Or have you ever had someone join your conversation from a nearby table? Here's what happened during a Zoom fellowship gathering.

Besides leading my own Warrior Fellowship, I also was attending an online fellowship via Zoom that was hosted by a dear sister in Denton, Texas. Those gatherings became a sacred space for me; it was where I learned the power of hosting with humility, praying in unity, and worshiping as one body.

Each session deepened my understanding that fellowship isn't just about meeting together; it's about encountering God's presence collectively. My heart had become softer, and I was desiring to see her group succeed. She started at 7:00 pm on Friday evening. My husband and I showed up faithfully every week. It was a very small gathering. We enjoyed the intimacy and the ability to support our sister in Christ.

One of the first times we were on, I had been giving my testimony of how I found a living God in the rooms of Alcoholics Anonymous. Without even knowing it, there was a man sitting a few seats away from where their fellowship had set up in the coffee shop. While eavesdropping on the fellowship's conversation, this gentleman was instantly convicted by my testimony. He asked the group for prayer and then gave his life to Jesus that very night. Afterwards, I watched a Coffee Talk Session that Dr. Kevin did, and he said, "The Lord told me that people want to be at the table next to you in a coffee shop and listen in on your conversation, and that's where you're going." Glory to God!

During the two years we attended this fellowship, people came and went. There was a woman by the name of Dixie who started attending in 2022. She had a guitar, and she became the group's minstrel. She had a powerful anointing and had the gift of faith. I wound up inviting her to the fellowship I had started on Sunday afternoon. She always brought her guitar and was eager to worship before the lesson began. Dixie and I became close friends because we had the same heart and mind. We encouraged one another daily. Dixie talked me into starting my own podcast on YouTube. When we prayed together, we saw mountains move. We would sing in tongues together until eventually we both heard the angels chiming in. It was the closest thing to an upper room experience I had ever encountered.

The Lord sent me Dixie just in the nick of time. I had become battle-weary, and my fire had started to dim. We all go through seasons of growth and change. She was the comic relief I needed. She reminded me not to take myself so seriously. We finally met in person at one of Dr. Kevin's conferences in Austin, Texas. We had the time of our lives. These memories I will cherish forever. Talk about being drunk in the Spirit!

Dixie began having shortness of breath in June 2023. She went in for a checkup and found out she had a large growth on top of her heart. Her surgeon removed the growth, but Dixie passed away in her home a few weeks later from an embolism.

My world turned upside down. I know in my heart that the Lord allowed me to meet this wonderful soul just when I needed her. I also know today that she is in the best possible place imaginable. The Father blessed me by allowing me to see her in a dream shortly after her passing. She pulled up to my home in a fancy car and got out, saying, "Get dressed because we are going dancing!" The Lord is so kind and merciful. That dream allowed me to find peace and closure. Once again, the Father was so mighty to spare me the pain and grief of losing a loved one.

> *So death, tell me, where is your victory? Tell me death, where is your sting?*
>
> **—1 Corinthians 15:55 TPT**

I am fully convinced there is none. When we lose the fear of death and of dying, we become unstoppable.

A few months ago, I was spending time with the Father. Soaking in my favorite place, I was relaxed, and I suddenly got very quiet. There was no one home at the time. There was a sacred silence. In the spirit I could hear a symphony playing. It was as clear and as real as could be. Then the Lord directed me to some old AA literature I had been saving. "Turn to page ten," I heard the Spirit say. I jumped up to go find my book and quickly turned to page ten. There it was in black and white.

The author was recollecting one of his childhood memories about his grandfather, trying to convince him that there really is a God. "His insistence that the spheres really had their music" was right there in Chapter 1 of the "Big Book" of Alcoholics Anonymous.[10] This teaching I received twenty-two years earlier would become the foundation of a new life—one in which I am no longer in charge. I had made an earnest decision to give God my will and my life. I came to God with an honest and humble desire to reconstruct my house. I allowed Him to knock down the preexisting structure and to begin rebuilding me from ground zero. I launched into a personal housecleaning, which meant I would have to go back in time to discover all the lies, ideas, and beliefs that blocked off the sunlight of God's Spirit. I agreed to follow directions.

---

10. *Alcoholics Anonymous*, "Big Book," 4th edition (Alcoholic Anonymous World Services, inc., 2001), 10.

Dr. Kevin often says, "There are no suggestion boxes in Heaven." This is true. There are no gray areas. It is black and white for me today. Either God is everything, or He is nothing. I chose to let down my guard and let the God of the universe, Yahweh, take complete control of my life. It was a fairly simple process, but it wasn't easy.

One weekend, while attending a supernatural conference in Bloomington, Illinois, I was reminded of how little I do know. The five speakers brought so much revelation and wisdom—it was mind-blowing. I love to be in the corporate anointing because we never know what spiritual food will be served. I love a good smorgasbord. I was also reminded that you are never too old to start dreaming again. There are no expiration dates on our dreams. One of the speakers there was in his mid-eighties, and he was the most on fire of them all. I hadn't planned on going to this conference, but my husband encouraged me to go because my very good friend was putting it on and he felt that I could be of service.

The night before I left, I had a dream of a blue blouse dangling in midair, and the Spirit said, "Come back soon because there's something I want to give you." I was thrilled. I was so busy that week, trying to get things packed for my trip that I never really made any time to sit quietly with the Lord. I made up my mind that in Bloomington I would attend the sessions but spend as much time alone in my room as possible.

Once I arrived at Bloomington's airport, it felt very refreshing to be back where this all began. The excitement and expectancy rose so high in my spirit. After settling into my room, I noticed I had a message on the hotel phone. It turned out to be from a friend from Georgia, Barry Wright, whom we affectionately call Dr. Barry. He had attended several of our online fellowships. In fact, we had been in the same Bible college at one point. It turns out that he was there attending the conference. He saved me a seat next to him.

During an intermission, while combing the book table, Dr. Barry approached me. "I want to thank you for all the love you and Doug pour out on Sundays," he said. He then explained that he received an impartation of love during our fellowship and that it was so powerful, his wife felt it. Whatever was imparted to him during our Bible study was enough to cause his wife to feel it and let her guard down. I was so touched by his sharing this story. The Father's love is powerful, no doubt. But to know our fellowship was the vehicle for that transfer of love was overwhelming.

Sometimes we can go through the motions and things become a habit. It's in those times that we don't see all that is being poured out. It was just one more reminder to pay close attention to the flock I was feeding. Now I am more attentive to the needs and prayers of the small group I have been blessed to assist Warrior Notes in stewarding.

I know the realm of the spirit is broad and inclusive. I have also come to understand that the road is very narrow. When I first got sober, I had several dreams of coming up to a gate or sometimes a glass door. I would get down on the floor and try to fit my head through the very small opening to enter. I realize, now, that those were dreams depicting the narrow way.

In my adolescence and young adult years, it was as if I was invincible. I didn't have much regard for others and especially was unaware of the world around me. If Kim had what she wanted and needed, then everything was just peachy.

Things are completely opposite these days, thanks be to God. He has allowed me to see the bigger picture. Although each of us is only one individual person, we have the power living inside of us that can affect an entire nation. What we do and say matters.

Just a few weeks ago, I dreamed of a man wearing a standard-issue prison uniform, and he was retrieving his personal effects. He turned and faced me and breathed a sigh of relief. He was exhausted. I embraced him and could feel his pain. Then, I woke up. I didn't recognize him as someone I knew personally.

Later that same week, I was watching the news. There was the man's picture. They were telling his story, except he was not the one being interviewed; it was his wife. She was asking the public and the media to please give him time to rest and recover. His name is Julian Assange. He is an Australian editor and activist who founded Wikileaks in 2006. Julian is what one might describe as a whistleblower or a conspiracy theorist. All I know is that for God to give me this in a dream, I am to pray for him and his family. I'm sure more will be revealed. It always is.

When I gave Jesus my "yes," I never could have fathomed what adventures would lie ahead for my family and me. I don't take matters of the Spirit lightly. While in Bloomington, Illinois, I heard Dean Braxton say, "You are not being humble; you are being rebellious!" He was referring to that thought you had from God to do something but then convinced yourself it was just your imagination. We talk ourselves out of God ideas all the time because we don't know the voice of the Father or we just don't believe we are worthy enough that God would want to talk to us. This is so far from the truth.

God doesn't have a speaking problem. We have a listening problem. Ninety percent of the church has been programmed to believe we need to hear from a prophet or a priest for God's guidance in our life, and this is just not true. There is no mediator now between God and man. Jesus is the way, the truth, and the life. Whoever follows Him will never walk in darkness but will have the light of life. (See John 14:6; 8:12.)

When I see a generation of souls floundering like fish in a fishbowl, it moves me to action. There are so many children and teens who are crying out for their Savior. Most of us are good givers but not a lot of us are good receivers. Being in ministry has taught me how to give and to receive, God's way.

If there is one thing that I have learned, it is to not judge my relationship with the Lord based on another's perception. One person may have spontaneous visitations and translations, but another might only receive such when he or she is praying or reading the Word. I am convinced that if you seek the Lord, you are sure to find Him. Some may take this as a casual suggestion, but it's not.

Lately I have noticed an influx of podcasts about near-death experiences and people sharing their testimonies after visiting hell. That has not been my experience. My hell was right here on earth, while I was running the show.

If you are reading this book, then the Lord has hand-selected you for a purpose. Take it from someone who knows and understands. I have spent the last twenty-two years developing an intimate relationship with the Trinity, and that was after I made the decision to give God my will and my life in May 2003.

Relationships take time to grow and flourish. It rarely happens overnight. I made a conscious effort to seek Him with all I had in me. I was so tired of hitting dead-ends. I was tired of seeing the same old circumstances in my life, day after day. I knew there was more.

CONCLUSION

Do you really understand that the Father already loves you and wants to be in a relationship with you? You don't have to earn His love. He loved you before the foundations of the world were formed.

I personally had to undo a lot of religious dogma. I had to throw away the man-made manual and pick up the real thing. These truths are not taught in church these days. The true church model was hijacked centuries ago. But that's another book.

Thankfully, along my journey with the Lord, someone shared with me the "Set Aside Prayer." I would like to share this special prayer with you.

> God, today help me to set aside everything I think I know about You, everything I think I know

> about myself, everything I think I know about others, and everything I think I know about my own recovery so that I may have an open mind and a new experience with all these things. Please help me to see the truth.[11]

A key to having an open mind and experiencing greater things of the Lord is to get rid of the fear of man and replace it with a healthy fear of the Lord. This is what is missing from the body of Christ as a whole. For example, children who are taught to respect their father show a noticeable difference in behavior. A healthy fear of the Lord is full of respect, honor, and regard.

You must become willing to believe that God wants to speak to you. A loving Father longs to communicate with His children. I have seen and have tasted the goodness of the Lord (see Psalm 34:8). My prayer for you is that you will lay it all down for Him. Put aside any false ideas that may have been given to you in your youth or even recently. Take up His yoke. He is gentle and kind. He only wants good for you. It doesn't matter how far down the scale you have gone; His arm is not too short. God is so intimately aware of each one of us. He has tailored every experience you will ever have.

If there is one thing I've learned, it is that our perception means everything. It will drive all your decisions. Once I aligned my mind with the mind of Christ, I could believe for the impossible.

---

11. Dr. Paul Greene, "The Set Aside Prayer," Manhattan Center for Cognitive Behavioral Therapy, website, October 19, 2020, https://manhattancbt.com/set-aside-prayer/.

The devil sold us a lie. The misconception was that we are alone and powerless. This is only true for the soul that has not been renewed. Once submitted to the will of God, power flows in and through us exactly where it is needed.

The question is, will you agree with God? I believe He has something better for all of us. I had to learn to get myself ready for it. As I mentioned before, learning to pass the test of waiting for God's guidance is no simple feat. We can't start praying while we are being thrown into the trenches. We all must learn how to walk in two realms if we are to live victoriously in this life.

There comes a moment in every soul's journey when the quiet whisper of eternity calls us to remember who we truly are—and whose we are.

Humbling myself and following the well-worn paths of those who had walked before me awakened me to the unseen. These tactics taught me to be still. To listen. To clear the noise of the mind and open the door of the heart.

At first, I was blind to the sacred weight of what I was entering into. I didn't yet see how each moment spent in prayer and meditation was planting seeds in the soil of my spirit. But over time—through seasons of silence, surrender, and seeking—those quiet seeds began to bloom into a new life rooted in the divine.

What I thought was a small offering of time became a deep investment in eternity. Every prayer, every breath of surrender, was a deposit into a spiritual treasury that now sustains me in ways I could never have imagined.

God, in His infinite love, has given us the freedom to choose. But freedom demands responsibility. We are invited, not forced, to walk the narrow path, to seek the hidden manna, to enter into communion with the Holy.

> *. . . choose this day whom you will serve. . . .*
>
> **—Joshua 24:15 ESV**

There is more. There is always more. But it begins with your choice.

Will you follow the voice that calls from beyond the veil? Will you fan the fire inside into a burning flame?

SALVATION PRAYER

Heavenly Father,

I come before You right now—undone, awakened, and fully surrendered.

I lay my life at Your feet. I release my will, my plans, my pride, and my control. I hold nothing back.

I confess that I am a sinner. I repent. Wash me clean and forgive me completely.

I believe that Jesus Christ died on the cross for my sins, that He rose in victory, and that He alone holds the keys to Heaven and hell. I declare that He is the way, the truth, and the life.

Jesus, come into my heart—take the throne of my life. Break what must be broken, and remake me according to Your purpose. I surrender fully to You.

Fill me now with Your Holy Spirit. Lead me, guide me, and empower me to walk in the path You have prepared for me from this day forward. Let my life bring You glory.

I boldly confess before Heaven and before men that Jesus Christ is my Lord and Savior.

In the mighty and saving name of Jesus, Amen.

ABOUT THE AUTHOR

Dr. **Kimberly Paz-Frazee** is a dynamic and anointed minister of the Gospel, ignited with a passion to see lives transformed by the power of God. Her journey began in the most unexpected of places—within the rooms of Alcoholics Anonymous—where she encountered the redemptive love of Jesus Christ after reaching a deep moral and spiritual low. From that point forward, her life has been marked by radical transformation and divine purpose.

In April 2018, Kimberly experienced a life-altering visitation from the Spirit of God that launched her into a new dimension of spiritual authority and revelation. Since then, she has walked boldly in the supernatural, with a growing sensitivity to the voice of God and an ability to discern future events both personally and prophetically for others.

Driven by love and a deep commitment to serving others, Kimberly lives by a simple yet powerful code: love in action. She is a multifaceted believer, unafraid to venture into spiritual depths that many shy away from. Her ministry is not confined to tradition or religion—it is one of radical obedience, raw authenticity, and relentless pursuit of God's heart.

Kimberly empowers others by sharing profound revelations born from seasons of struggle, surrender, and seeking more of God. Her teachings boldly address hard truths, challenge religious norms, and offer practical, Spirit-led insight into walking in both the natural and supernatural realms.

A fearless communicator and a passionate teacher, Kimberly is raising up a generation of believers equipped to hear God's voice clearly, walk in true freedom, and live out their divine calling with courage and clarity. Her message is simple, yet revolutionary: God's voice is real, His power is available, and His love changes everything.

Kimberly received her Doctorate in Divinity through Warrior Notes School of Ministry, is a licensed Chaplain, author, speaker and has served her community as a registered nurse for three decades. She resides in Mico, Texas with her husband and four children.

You can reach Kimberly at: fanitintoflame7@gmail.com

www.ingramcontent.com/pod-product-compliance
Lightning Source LLC
LaVergne TN
LVHW012332100826
845148LV00017B/2122

9781663101884